A SOLDIER'S STORY

OF THE

SIEGE OF VICKSBURG,

FROM THE DIARY OF

OSBORN H. OLDROYD,

(LATE SERGEANT CO. E, 20TH OHIO.
EDITOR "LINCOLN MEMORIAL ALBUM.")

WITH

CONFEDERATE ACCOUNTS FROM AUTHENTIC SOURCES, AND AN
INTRODUCTION BY BREVET MAJ.-GEN. M. F. FORCE.

———————

ILLUSTRATED

WITH PORTRAITS AND APPROPRIATE ENGRAVINGS,

———————

———————

SPRINGFIELD, ILL.:
PUBLISHED FOR THE AUTHOR,
1885.

H. W. ROKKER,

PRINTER, BINDER AND STEREOTYPER,

Springfield, Ill.

A SOLDIER'S STORY

OF THE

SIEGE OF VICKSBURG

FROM THE DIARY OF

OSBORN H. OLDROYD

Digital Scanning and Publishing is a leader in the electronic republication of historical books and documents. We publish many of our titles as eBooks, paperback and hardcover editions. DSI is committed to bringing many traditional and well-known books back to life, retaining the look and feel of the original work.

Trade Paperback ISBN: 1-58218-841-6

©2009 DSI Digital Reproduction
First DSI Printing: December 2009

Published by Digital Scanning Inc. Scituate, MA 02066
781-545-2100 http://www.Digitalscanning.com and
http://www.PDFLibrary.com

GENERAL CONTENTS.

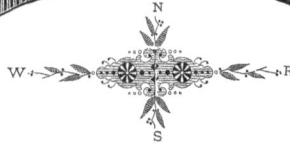

DEDICATION.

To the boys that fought the battles of the Civil War, this volume is dedicated. The pictures of their daily life in camp, on the march, and in battle, were drawn upon the field of action. May the memory of those deeds never perish, but ever remain fresh, as a part of the record of the historic times which knit us together as

COMRADES.

PREFACE.

I GRASPED a Harper's Ferry musket and joined Company E, 20th Ohio Regiment of Volunteers, at Camp Chase, in Ohio, October 15, 1861. Though but nineteen years of age, and in delicate health, I soon became acclimated, and took part in nearly all the operations of my regiment from the engagement at Fort Donelson to the close of the war, when I was mustered out, on the 19th of July, 1865, in the same camp in which I had enlisted.

The scenes described in this little volume were put in writing at the front. They are not sketches from fancy, produced by the aid of memory after the lapse of twenty years, but each day's march, battle, or life in the camp, was recorded upon the spot—now, at the close of a hard day's march; again, when tired and hungry after a hotly contested battle; and again, in the camp, while the cross-firing of the contending lines made it impossible to find a place secure enough to write down the day's transactions. I have brushed the powder of a bursting shell off my paper, and changed my position in order to escape the range of the enemy's guns. Under such difficulties my diary of the siege of Vicksburg was kept.

All I claim for this volume is, that it is a simple and straight-forward story of the life of a soldier in the ranks. It is hoped that it may serve the purpose of refreshing the memory of those who fought the battles and endured the hardships of our great struggle. If it will only serve to kindle that patriotism in the heart of some youth, that will enable him to spring to arms at his country's call, in defense of the Nation's honor, as did the boys of '61, the author shall feel abundantly paid for his labor.

It is my pleasure to cherish none but the best of feelings to-ward those in gray who met us on the field of battle. The men in the ranks, on both sides, always met, outside of the battle

ground, with the best of feeling for one another; and now that
the war is over, they can certainly shake hands most heartily
across the bloody chasm.

Our commanding officers will always be remembered as brave
soldiers and devoted patriots, and they won the hearts of all the
men in the ranks.

In closing this preface, I wish to express my most cordial
thanks to those who have kindly loaned their portraits to be
engraved for this volume.

"With malice toward none, with charity for all,"

I subscribe myself,

OSBORN H. OLDROYD.

LINCOLN MANSION, SPRINGFIELD, ILL.,
JULY 4TH, 1885.

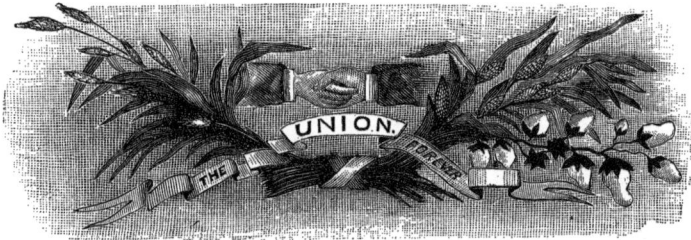

INTRODUCTION.

ISTORY treats of men in masses. It does not undertake to portray individuals, except leaders and men of prominence. The histories of our civil war tell of the movements of armies and acts of generals. But the war was a popular uprising. It was carried on by the people. It cannot be understood without a knowledge of the enlisted men,—how they felt, how they lived, what they thought.

The diary kept by an enlisted man through the Vicksburg campaign is a valuable contribution to such knowledge. The writer, OSBORN H. OLDROYD, while yet not of age, was appointed Fifth Sergeant of Company E, 20th Ohio, just before the battle of Raymond. His company went into the battle under the command of the Second Lieutenant. Early in the engagement the lieutenant was shot through the neck; the First Sergeant was killed, and soon young Oldroyd was in command of the company. He gallantly held the responsible post till the close of the battle. Intelligent, trusty, honorable, his narrative may be depended upon as a faithful description of what he saw.

M. F. FORCE.

CINCINNATI, OHIO, 1885.

PERSONAL REMINISCENCE.

MAY 1ST, 1863.—Logan's Division, to which we belonged, embarked on transports, that had passed the batteries at Vicksburg and Grand Gulf, last night, about two miles below the latter place, where we had marched down the Louisiana levee to meet the boats. Crossing the Mississippi river, we landed at Bruinsburg, and left that place this forenoon at 10 o'clock, marching twelve miles over dusty roads and through a hilly and broken country. Although the boys were tired, their minds were diverted

with the scenery of a new State. After crossing the great Mississippi, we bade farewell to Louisiana and its alligators, and are now inhaling the fragrance and delightful odors of Mississippi flowers. Arriving near Port Gibson about dark, found that the advance of McClernand's corps had defeated the enemy,

who had marched out from Vicksburg to check our army. The
fight was quite spirited, and the rebels hotly and bravely contested every foot of ground, but they were overpowered, as they
will be in every engagement they have with us. Having only two
days' rations in our haversacks, guess we will have to eat rather
sparingly of them, for our wagon train is not on the road. Should
rations run short, we will have to forage off the country; but even
the supplies from that source will not feed Grant's large army.
We were well satisfied, however, that the stars and stripes were
victorious, in this battle, without our assistance. We did not
smell the battle afar off, but heard cannonading through the day,
and fully expected to take a hand in it. When we stopped, as we
supposed, for the night, our Colonel drew the regiment into line,
and said Gen. McPherson had asked him if his regiment was too
wearied to follow the retreating enemy. When the question was
put to the men, every one wanted to go, and started on the trail
with the swiftness of fresh troops, marching as rapidly as possible until 10 o'clock, then camped in a ravine for the night.
During this rapid movement, we did some skirmishing. The
Confederate army had retreated, and we made the tail of it fly
over the road pretty lively.

"The battle was fought, and the victory won;
Three cheers for the Union! the work was well done.'

Porter's Gun-boats in front of Grand Gulf.

MAY 2ND.—As the sun peeped over the eastern horizon, we slipped out of camp and went our way rejoicing. Oh, how beautiful the morning; calm and pleasant, with the great variety of birds warbling, as though all was peace and quiet. When camping in the darkness of night, our surroundings astonish us in the broad day light. We scarcely know our next door neighbor until the morning light gleams upon him. While waiting orders to move, many thousand troops passed to the front, so I think our regiment will see another day pass with unbroken ranks. We have the very best fighting material in our regiment, and a, e ever ready for action, but are not particularly "spoiling for a fight." Our turn will come, as it did at Fort Donelson, Shiloh and many other fields of glory. It is quite common to hear soldiers who have never seen the first fight say they are afraid they will never get any of the glories of this war. They never "spoil" for the second fight, but get glory enough in the first to last them. When our regiment was living upon soft bread and luxuries of sweet things from home, while camped in the rear of Covington, Kentucky, we thought that the war would be over and our names not be spread upon our banners as the victors in a battle. There is glory enough for all. We stopped awhile in Port Gibson, and the boys found a lot of blank bank currency of different denominations, upon the Port Gibson bank. They signed some of them, and it is quite common to see a private of yesterday a bank president to-day. This may not become a circulating medium to a very great extent, but it is not at all likely that it will be refused by the inhabitants along our route when tendered in payment for corn-bread, sweet potatoes, etc. In the afternoon we stopped awhile, and taking advantage of the halt made coffee, which is generally done, whether it is noon or not. There is a wonderful stimulant in a cup of coffee, and as we require a great nerve tonic, coffee is eagerly sought after. Dick Hunt, of Company G, and Tom McVey, of Co. B, discovered a poor lonely confederate chicken by the roadside. By some hen strategem it had eluded the eyes of at least ten thousand Yankees, but when the 20th Ohio came along the searching eyes of these two members espied its place of concealment. They chased it under an outhouse, which was on stilts, as a great many of the southern houses are. Dick being rather the fleetest crawled under the house and secured the feathered prize, but Tom seeing his defeat in not securing a "preacher's dinner," found a coffee-pot under another corner of the house, which he brought to daylight, and it proved to be full of silver coin mostly dollars. These he traded off to the boys for paper, as he could not carry his load. How foolish it is for the Southern people to flee and leave their beautiful property to the foe. We only want something to eat. There are some who would apply the torch to a deserted home, that would not do so if the owners remained in it. It is quite common here to build the chimneys on the outside of the houses, and I have noticed them still standing where the house had been burned. The march to-day, towards Black River, has been a very pleasant one. I suppose Grant knows where he is taking us to, for we don't, not having had any communications with him lately upon the subject.

MAY 3D.—Called up early, and off on the march. Received a mail to-day, which was a welcome visitor to many, as it is the first one for some time. May they come oftener, and to every soldier. One poor fellow, who did not receive a letter, declared his girl had grown tired of him, and probably taken a beau at home. Another sympathized with him in the disappointment, and offered to let him read the letter he had received from his girl, who was aiding and encouraging him with her prayers. Pursued the enemy through the day, and were at their heels all the time, and at evening caught sight of them crossing Hankinson's Ferry, on Black River. We made a rapid charge upon them, firing as we ran, while DeGolier's battery shelled them. Some few were shot while crossing, the bridge. I suppose they have retreated to Vicksburg, as they are on a direct road to that place. After driving the enemy across the temporary bridge, we closed up business for the night, and sought our blankets.

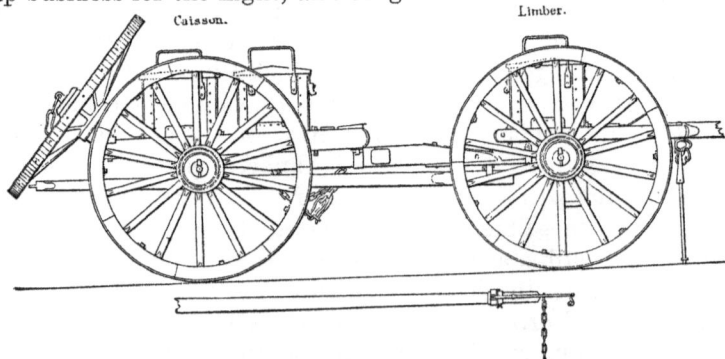

Caisson.   Limber.

Field Gun-Carriage.

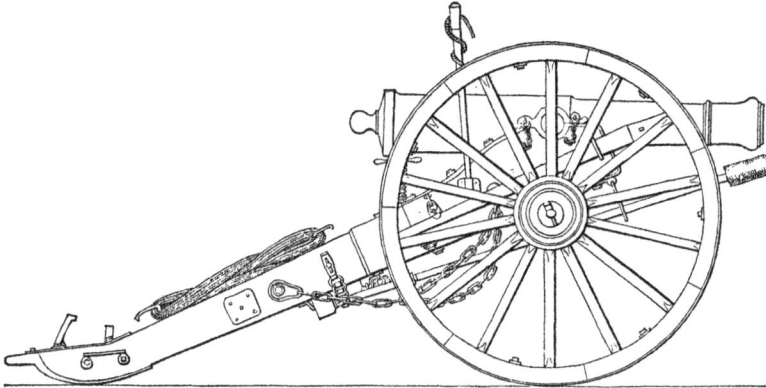

12-pound Howitzer.

MAY 4TH.—Early this morning the rebels planted a battery in the woods on the opposite side of the river, and sent shot and shell crashing into our camp. DeGolier's battery was soon in position, and silenced them before any damage was done. I hope DeGolier and his battery will be with us through all our engagements, for a braver man never lived. Some of his artillerymen said, he would rise up in his sleep, last night, and say, "give them canister, boys!"

I was detailed with a squad to patrol the river bank, and, in doing so, came in collision with the enemy. Some of the boys could not resist the temptation to take a swim. They did not think of the danger, until they were fired upon. When they went in, they complained of the water being cold; but they were not in long before it became too hot for them. They got out of that stream remarkably quick, and some did not stop to get their clothing, but flew for camp as naked as they were born. They did not know but the woods were full of rebels. A soldier's life has its share of fun as well as of the sad and marvelous.

I suppose this is considered an unsafe place to leave unguarded, so we remain another day.

MAY 5TH.—We were annoyed some little through the night, by the rebels firing, but they didn't hit anybody. Two regiments of infantry with some cavalry crossed the river for a little scout. I do not think there are many rebels over there, but what few there are, ought to be whipped. They will have to fall back at the approach of our men, but that is easily done, and, when our forces return, they will be right back firing from behind the trees.

The army is marching on around Vicksburg, and we are very anxious to take our place in this grand column. We are quite tired of the duties assigned us here, and have had orders to move several times, which were as often countermanded.

Had chicken for dinner. Uncle Sam doesn't furnish chickens in his bill of fare, but they *will* get into the camp kettle. We have to be very saving of the regular rations, consequently must look outside for extras—chickens, ham, sweet potatoes, etc., all taste good. I walked down the river a short distance, viewing the scenery, when a bullet flew through the trees not far from my head. I looked across the river from whence it came, but could not see anybody. Did not stay there long, but got back to camp, where I felt safer.

Our camp is in the bottom, close to the river bank. The enemy at Grand Gulf spiked their cannon and retreated to Vicksburg. If that place could not be taken by the gun-boats on the river in front, the infantry marching in their rear made them hustle out in a hurry. When the people in Vicksburg see their retreating troops returning to the town they went out to protect, they will think Grant's marching around them means something.

While writing a few letters to-day I was amused to notice the various attitudes taken by the boys while writing. One wrote on a drum-head, another on his cartridge-box; one used a board and several wrote on the top of a battery caisson. These letters would be more highly appreciated by the recipients if the circumstances under which they were prepared were realized.

MAY 6TH.—This day has been a hot one, but as our duties have not been of an arduous nature we have sought the shade and kept quiet. While in camp, the boys very freely comment upon our destination, and give every detail of progress a general overhauling. The ranks of our volunteer regiments were filled at the first call for troops. That call opened the doors of both rich and poor, and out sprang merchant, farmer, lawyer, physician and mechanics of every calling, whose true and loyal hearts all beat in unison for their country. The first shot that struck Sumpter's wall sent an electric shot to every loyal breast, and to-day we have in our ranks material for future captains, colonels and generals, who before this war is ended will be sought out and honored.

It can not be possible that we are to be kept at this place much longer, for it is not very desirable as a permanent location. Of course we are here for some purpose, and I suppose that to be to prevent the enemy from assailing our line of supplies. As they are familiar with the country they can annoy us exceedingly without much loss to themselves. But after we have captured Vicksburg, and the history of Grant's movements is known, we shall then understand why we guarded Hankinson's Ferry so long. One of the boys said he thought Mr. Hankinson owed us something nice for taking such good care of his ferry for him. The variety of comments and opinions expressed in camp by the men is very curious. Some say we are going to surround Vicksburg, others think Grant is feeling for the enemy's weakest point there to strike him, and one cool head remarked that it was all right wherever we went while Grant was leading, for he had never known defeat. Confidence in a good general stiffens a soldier— a rule that ought to work both ways. Surely no leader ever had more of the confidence of those he led than General Grant. He is not as social as McPherson, Sherman, Logan and some others, but seems all the while careful of the comfort of his men, with an eye single to success. Great responsibilities, perhaps, suppress his social qualities, for the present; for each day presents new obstacles to be met and overcome without delay. The enemy are doing all they can to hinder us, but let Grant say *forward*, and we obey.

Unable to sleep last night, I strolled about the camp awhile. Cause of my wakefulness, probably too much chicken yesterday. I appeared to be the only one in such a state, for the rest were

"Lost in heavy slumbers,
    Free from toil and strife,
Dreaming of their dear ones,
    Home and child and wife;
Tentless they are lying,
    While the moon shines bright.
Sleeping in their blankets,
    Beneath the summer's night."

MAY 7TH.—Our company detailed and reported this morning at headquarters for picket duty, but not being needed, returned to camp. Were somewhat disappointed, for we preferred a day on picket by way of change.

Pickets are the eyes of the army and the terror of those who live in close proximity to their line. Twenty-four hours on picket is hardly ever passed without some good foraging.

We broke camp at ten o'clock A. M., and very glad of it. After a pleasant tramp of ten miles we reached Rocky Springs. Here we have good, cold spring water, fresh from the bosom of the hills.

We have met several of the men of this section who have expressed surprise at the great number of troops passing. They think there must be a million of "you'ns" coming down here. We have assured them they have not seen half of our army. To our faces these citizens seem good Union men, but behind our backs, no doubt their sentiments undergo a change. Probably they were among those who fired at us, and will do it again as soon as they dare. I have not seen a regular acknowledged rebel since we crossed the river, except those we have seen in their army. They may well be surprised at the size of our force, for this Vicksburg expedition is indeed a big thing, and I am afraid the people who were instrumental in plunging this country headlong into this war have not yet realized what evils they have waked up. They are just beginning to open their eyes to war's career of devastation. They must not complain when they go out to the barnyard in the morning and find a hog or two missing at roll-call, or a few chickens less to pick corn and be picked in turn for the pot. I think these southern people will be benefited by the general diffusion of information which our army is introducing; and after the war new enterprise and better arts will follow—the steel plow, for instance, in place of the bull-tongue or old *root* that has been in use here so long to scratch the soil. The South must suffer, but out of that suffering will come wisdom.

MAY 8TH.—We were ready to continue our march, but were not ordered out. Some white citizens came into camp to see the "Yankees," as they call us. Of course they do not know the meaning of the term, but apply it to all Union soldiers. They will think there are plenty of Yankees on this road if they watch it. The country here looks desolate. The owners of the plantations are "dun gone," and the fortunes of war have cleared away the fences. One of the boys foraged to-day and brought into camp, in his blanket, a variety of vegetables—and nothing is so palatable to us now as a vegetable meal, for we have been living a little too long on nothing but bacon. Pickles taste first-rate. I always write home for pickles, and I've a lady friend who makes and sends me, when she can, the best kind of "ketchup." There is nothing else I eat that makes me *catch up* so quick. There is another article we learn to appreciate in camp, and that is news-papers—something fresh to read. The boys frequently bring in reading matter with their forage. Almost anything in print is better than nothing. A novel was brought in to-day, and as soon as it was caught sight of a score or more had engaged in turn the reading of it. It will soon be read to pieces, though handled as carefully as possible, under the circumstances. We can not get reading supplies from home down here. I know papers have been sent to me, but I never got them. The health of our boys is good, and they are brimful of spirits (not "commissary"). We are generally better on the march than in camp, where we are too apt to get lazy, and grumble; but when moving we digest almost anything. When soldiers get bilious, they can not be satis-fied until they are set in motion.

MAY 9TH.—Orders this morning to draw two days' rations, pack up and be ready to move at a moment's warning. We drew hard-tack, coffee, bacon, salt and sugar, and stored them in our haversacks. Some take great care so to pack the hard-tack that it will not dig into the side while marching, for if a corner sticks out too much anywhere, it is only too apt to leave its mark on the soldier. Bacon, too, must be so placed as not to grease the blouse or pants. I see many a bacon badge about me—generally in the region of the left hip. In filling canteens, if the covers get wet the moisture soaks through and scalds the skin. The tin cup or coffee-can is generally tied to the canteen or else to the blanket or haversack, and it rattles along the road, reminding one of the sound of the old cow coming home. All trifling troubles like these on the march may be easily forestalled by a little care, but care is something a soldier is not apt to take, and he too often packs his "grub" as hurriedly as he "bolts" it. We were soon ready to move, and filled our canteens with the best water we have had for months. We did not actually get our marching order, however, until near three o'clock P. M., so that being anxious to take fresh water with us, we had to empty and refill canteens several times. As we waited for the order, a good view was afforded us of the passing troops, and the bristling lines really looked as if there was war ahead.

O, what a grand army this is, and what a sight to fire the heart of a spectator with a speck of patriotism in his bosom. I shall never forget the scene of to-day, while looking back upon a mile

of solid columns, marching with their old tattered flags streaming
in the summer breeze, and hearkening to the firm tramp of their
broad brogans keeping step to the pealing fife and drum, or the
regimental bands discoursing "Yankee Doodle" or "The Girl I
Left Behind Me." I say it was a grand spectacle—but how different the scene when we meet the foe advancing to the strains of
"Dixie" and "The Bonny Blue Flag." True, I have no fears for
the result of such a meeting, for we are marching full of the
prestige of victory, while our foes have had little but defeat for
the last two years. There is an inspiration in the memory of
victory. Marching through this hostile country with large odds
against us, we have crossed the great river and wi l cut our way
through to Vicksburg, let what dangers may confront u≈. To
turn back we should be overwhelmed with hos s exulting on their
own native soil. These people can and will fight despera'ely, but
they cannot put a barrier in our way that we cannot pass.
Camped a little after dark.

MAY 10TH.—Left camp after dinner. Dinner generally means
noon, but our dinner-time on the march is quite irregular. Advanced unmolested till within about three miles of Utica, and
camped again at dark.

This forenoon my bunk-mate (Cal. Waddle) and I went to a
house near camp to get some corn bread, but struck the wrong
place, for we found the young mistress who had just been deserted by her negroes, all alone, crying, with but a scant allowance
of provisions left her. She had never learned to cook, and in
fact was a complete stranger to housework of any kind. Her
time is now at hand to learn the great lesson of humanity. There
has been a little too much idleness among these planters. But
although I am glad the negroes are free I don't like to see them
leaving a good home, for good homes some of them I know are
leaving. They have caught the idea from some unknown source
that freedom means fine dress, furniture, carriages and luxuries.
Little do they yet know of the scripture—"In the sweat of thy
face shalt thou eat bread." I am for the Emancipation Procla-
mation, but I do not believe in cheating them. This lady's hus-
band is a confederate officer now in Vicksburg, who told her when
he left she should never see a Yankee "down thar." Well, we
had to tell her we were "thar," though, and to our question what she
thought of us, after wiping her eyes her reply was we were very

nice looking fellows. We were not fishing for compliments, but we like to get their opinions at sight, for they have been led, apparently, to expect to find the Lincoln soldier more of a beast than human. At least such is the belief among the lower sort. Negroes and poor whites here seem to be on an equality, so far as education is concerned and the respect of the better classes. I have not seen a single school-house since I have been in Dixie, and I do not believe such a thing exists outside of their cities. But this war will revolutionize things, and among others I hope change this state of affairs for the better.

War is a keen analyzer of a soldier's character. It reveals in camp, on the march and in battle the true principles of the man better than they are shown in the every-day walks of life. Here he has a chance to throw off the vicious habits of the past, and take such a stand as to gain a lasting reputation for good, or, if he dies upon the field, the glory of his achievements, noble deeds and soldierly bearing in camp will live in the memory of his comrades. Every soldier has a personal history to make, which will be agreeable, or not, as he chooses. A company of soldiers are as a family; and, if every member of it does his duty towards the promotion of good humor, much will be done toward softening the hardships of that sort of life.

This is Sunday, and few seem to realize it. I would not have known it myself but for my diary. I said, "boys this is Sunday." Somebody asked, "how do you know it is?" I replied my diary told me. Another remarked, "you ought to tell us then when Sunday comes round so we can try to be a little better than on week days." While in regular camps we have had preaching by the Chaplains, but now that we are on the move that service is dispensed with, and what has become of the Chaplains now I am unable to say. Probably buying and selling cotton, for some of them are regular tricksters, and think more of filling their own pockets with greenbacks than the hearts of soldiers with the word of God.

MAY 11TH.—We drew two days' rations and marched till noon. My company, E, being detailed for rear guard, a very undesirable position. General Logan thinks we shall have a fight soon. I am not particularly anxious for one, but if it comes I will make my musket talk. As we contemplate a battle, those who have been spoiling for a fight cease to be heard. It does not even take the

The raid on the fence before going into camp.

smell of powder to quiet their nerves—a rumor being quite sufficient.

We have no means of knowing the number of troops in Vicksburg, but if they were well generaled and thrown against us at some particular point, the matter might be decided without going any further. If they can not whip us on our journey around their city, why do they not stay at home and strengthen their boasted position, and not lose so many men in battle to discourage the remainder? We are steadily advancing, and propose to keep on until we get them where they *can't* retreat. My fear is that they may cut our supply train, and then we should be in a bad fix. Should that happen and they get us real hungry, I am afraid short work would be made of taking Vicksburg.

Having seen the four great Generals of this department, shall always feel honored that I was a member of Force's 20th Ohio, Logan's Division, McPherson's Corps of Grant's Army. The expression upon the face of Grant was stern and care-worn, but determined. McPherson's was the most pleasant and courteous— a perfect gentleman and an officer that the 17th corps fairly worships. Sherman has a quicker and more dashing movement than some others, a long neck, rather sharp features, and altogether just such a man as might lead an army through the enemy's country. Logan is brave and does not seem to know what defeat means. We feel that he will bring us out of every fight victorious. I want no better or braver officers to fight under. I have often thought of the sacrifice that a General might make of his men in order to enhance his own *eclat*, for they do not always seem to display the good judgment they should. But I have no fear of a needless sacrifice of life through any mismanagement of this army.

MAY 12TH.—Roused up early and before daylight marched, the 20th in the lead. Now we have the honored position, and will probably get the first taste of battle. At nine o'clock slight skirmishing began in front, and at eleven we filed into a field on the right of the road, where another regiment joined us on our right, with two other regiments on the left of the road and a battery in the road itself. In this position our line marched down through open fields until we reached the fence, which we scaled and stacked arms in the edge of a piece of timber. No sooner had we done this than the boys fell to amusing themselves in

DeGolier's Battery going into action at the Battle of Raymond.

various ways, taking little heed of the danger about to be entered. A group here and there were employed in "euchre," for cards seem always handy enough where soldiers are. Another little squad was discussing the scenes of the morning. One soldier picked up several canteens, saying he would go ahead and see if he could fill them. Soon after he disappeared, he returned with a quicker pace and with but one canteen full, saying, when asked why he came back so quick—"while I was filling the canteen I heard a noise, and looking up discovered several Johnnies behind trees, getting ready to shoot, and I concluded I would retire at once and report." Meanwhile my bedfellow had taken from his pocket a small mirror and was combing his hair and moustache. Said some one to him, "Cal., you needn't fix up so nice to go into battle, for the rebs won't think any better of you for it."

Just here the firing began in our front, and we got orders: "Attention! Fall in—take arms—forward—double-quick, march!" And we moved quite lively, as the rebel bullets did likewise. We had advanced but a short distance—probably a hundred yards— when we came to a creek, the bank of which was high, but down we slid, and wading through the water, which was up to our knees, dropped upon the opposite side and began firing at will. We did not have to be told to shoot, for the enemy were but a hundred yards in front of us, and it seemed to be in the minds of both officers and men that this was the very spot in which to settle the question of our right of way. They fought desperately, and no doubt they fully expected to whip us early in the fight, before we could get reinforcements. There was no bank in front to protect my company, and the space between us and the foe was open and perfectly level. Every man of us knew it would be sure death to all to retreat, for we had behind us a bank seven feet high, made slippery by the wading and climbing back of the wounded, and where the foe could be at our heels in a moment. However, we had no idea of retreating, had the ground been twice as inviting; but taking in the situation only strung us up to higher determination. The regiment to the right of us was giving way, but just as the line was wavering and about to be hopelessly broken, Logan dashed up, and with the shriek of an eagle turned them back to their places, which they regained and held. Had it not been for Logan's timely intervention, who was continually riding up and down the line, firing the men with his own enthusiasm, our line would undoubtedly have been broken at some point. For two hours the contest raged furiously, but as man after man dropped dead or wounded, the rest were inspired the more firmly to hold fast their places and avenge the fallen. The creek was running red with precious blood spilt for our country. My bunk-

mate and I were kneeling side by side when a ball crashed through his brain, and he fell over with a mortal wound. With the assistance of two others I picked him up, carried him over the bank in our rear, and laid behind a tree, removing from his pocket, watch and trinkets, and the same little mirror that had helped him make his last toilet but a little while before. We then went back to our company after an absence of but a few minutes. Shot and shell from the enemy came over thicker and faster, while the trees rained bunches of twigs around us.

John Calvin Waddell, Corporal Co. E, 20th Ohio, killed May 12, 1863.

One by one the boys were dropping out of my company. The second lieutenant in command was wounded; the orderly sergeant dropped dead, and I find myself (fifth sergeant) in command of the handful remaining. In front of us was a reb in a red shirt, when one of our boys, raising his gun, remarked, "see me bring that red shirt down," while another cried out, "hold on, that is my man." Both fired, and the red shirt fell—it may be riddled by more than those two shots. A red shirt is, of course, rather too conspicuous on a battle field. Into another part of the line the enemy charged, fighting hand to hand, being too close to fire, and using the butts of their guns. But they were all

—2

Hand-to-hand conflict.

forced to give way at last, and we followed them up for a short distance, when we were passed by our own reinforcements coming up just as we had whipped the enemy. I took the roll-book from the pocket of our dead sergeant, and found that while we had gone in with thirty-two men, we came out with but sixteen—one-half of the brave little band, but a few hours before so full of hope and patriotism, either killed or wounded. Nearly all the survivors could show bullet marks in clothing or flesh, but no man left the field on account of wounds. When I told Colonel Force of our loss, I saw tears course down his cheeks, and so intent were his thoughts upon his fallen men that he failed to note the bursting of a shell above him, scattering the powder over his person, as he sat at the foot of a tree.

Although our ranks have been so thinned by to-day's battle our will is stronger than ever to march and fight on, and avenge the death of those we must leave behind. I am very sad on account of the loss of so many of my comrades, especially the one who bunked with me, and who had been to me like a brother, even sharing my load when it grew burdensome. He has fallen; may he sleep quietly under the shadows of those old oaks which looked down upon the struggle of to-day.

We moved up to the town of Raymond and there camped. I suppose this will be named the battle of Raymond. The citizens had prepared a good dinner for the rebels on their return from victory, but as they actually returned from defeat they were in too much of a hurry to enjoy it. It is amusing now to hear the boys relating their experiences going into battle. All agree that to be under fire without the privilege of returning it is uncomfortable—a feeling which soon wears off when their own firing begins. I suppose the sensations of our boys are as varied as their individualities. No matter how brave a man may be, when he first faces the muskets and cannon of an enemy he is seized with a certain degree of fear, and to some it becomes an occasion of an involuntary but very sober review of their past lives. There is now little time for meditation; scenes change rapidly; he quickly resolves to do better if spared, but when afterward marching from a victorious field such good resolutions are easily forgotten. I confess, with humble pleasure, that I have never neglected to ask God's protection when going into a fight, nor thanking him for the privilege of coming out again alive. The only thought that troubles me is that of falling into an unknown grave.

The battle to-day opened very suddenly, and when DeGolier's battery began to thunder, while the infantry fire was like the pattering of a shower, some cooks, happening to be surprised near the front, broke for the rear carrying their utensils. One of them with a kettle in his hand, rushing at the top of his speed, met General Logan, who halted him, asking where he was going, when the cook piteously cried, "Oh General, I've got no gun, and such a snapping and cracking as there is up yonder I never heard before." The General let him pass to the rear.

*Thomas Runyan, of Company A, was wounded by a musket ball which entered the right eye, and passing behind the left forced it out upon his cheek. As the regiment passed, I saw him lying by the side of the road, tearing the ground in his death struggle.

MAY 13TH.—Up early, and on the march to Jackson, as we suppose.

I dreamed of my bunk-mate last night. Wonder if his remains will be put where they can be found, for I would like, if I ever get the chance, to put a board with his name on it at the head of his grave. When we enlisted we all paired off, each selecting his comrade—such a one as would be congenial and agreeable to him—and as yesterday's battle broke a good many

*NOTE.—When the regiment was being mustered out in July, 1865, Thomas Runyan, who had been left for dead, visited the regiment. He said he came "to see the boys." He was, of course, totally blind.

such bonds, new ties have been forming,—as the boys say, new couples are getting married. If married people could always live as congenial and content as two soldiers sleeping under the same blanket, there would be more happiness in the world. I shall await the return of one of the wounded.

We arrived at Clinton after dark, a place on the Jackson and Vicksburg railroad. Yesterday a train ran through, the last that will ever be run by confederates. The orders are to destroy the road here in each direction. We expected to have to fight for this spot, but instead we took possession unmolested. "Cotton is king," and finding a good deal here, we have made our beds of it.

MAY 14TH.—Started again this morning for Jackson. When within five miles of the city we heard heavy firing. It has rained hard to-day and we have had both a wet and muddy time, pushing at the heavy artillery and provision wagons accompanying us when they stuck in the mud. The rain came down in perfect torrents. What a sight! Ambulances creeping along at the side of the track— artillery toiling in the deep ruts, while Generals with their aids and orderlies splashed mud and water in every direction in passing. We were all wet to the skin, but plodded on patiently, for the love of country.

When within a few miles of Jackson, the news reached us that Sherman had slipped round to the right and captured the place, and the shout that went up from the men on the receipt of that news was invigorating to them in the midst of trouble. I think they could have been heard in Jackson. Sherman's army at the right and McPherson in our immediate front, with one desperate charge we ran without stopping till we reached the town. The flower of the confederate forces, the pride of the Southern States who had never yet known defeat, came up to Jackson last night to help demolish Grant's army, but for once they failed. Veterans of Georgia stationed as reserves were also forced to yield in dismay, and never stopped retreating till they had passed far south of the Capital which they had striven so valiantly to defend. To-night the stars and stripes float proudly over the cupola of the seat of government of Mississippi—and if my own regiment has not had a chance to-day to cover itself with glory it has with mud.

I shall not soon forget the conversation I have had with a wounded rebel. He said that his regiment last night was full of men who had never before met us, and who felt sure it would be easy to whip us. How they were deceived! He said part of his regiment was behind a hedge fence, where they felt comparatively safe, but the Yankees jumped right over without stopping, and swept everything before them. I never saw finer looking men than the killed and wounded rebels of to-day, and with the smooth face of one of them, lying in a garden mortally wounded, I was so taken, that I eased his thirst with a drink from my own canteen. His piteous glance at me at that time I shall never forget. It is on the battle field and among the dead and dying we get to know each other better—nay, even our own selves. Administering to a stranger, we think of his mother's love, as dear to him as our own to us. When the fight is over, away all bitterness. Let us leave with the foe some tokens of good will, that, when the cruel war at last is over, may be kindly remembered. I trust our enemies may yet be led to hail in good faith the return of peace and the restoration of the Union. This is a domestic war, the saddest of all, being fought between those whose hearts should be as brothers; and when it is at an end, may those hearts again throb together beneath the folds of the flag that once waved for defence over their sires and themselves —a flag whose proud motto will be, "peace on earth and good will to men."

Some of the boys went down into the city to view our new possession. It seems ablaze, but I trust only public property is being destroyed, or such as might aid and comfort the enemy here-
after.

I am very tired, and of course can easily get excused, so I will
go to my bed on the ground.

MAY 15TH.—The familiar "Attention, battalion!" was heard
from our Colonel, when we marched back upon the same road
that had led us to Jackson, camping as usual at dark. We
passed through Clinton, and the inhabitants were surprised to
see us returning so soon, for they fully expected to hear of our
being defeated and driven back. But they did not know our
metal. The last few days have been full of excitement, and
although we have marched and fought hard, and lost some of our
best men, besides getting tired and hungry ourselves, we are more
resolved than ever to keep the ball rolling. The thinner our ranks
are made by fighting and disease, the closer together the remnants are brought. We shall close up the ranks and press forward until the foe is vanquished. Soldiers grow more friendly as
they are brought better to realize the terrible ravages of war. As
Colonel Force called us to "Attention!" this morning, one of the
boys remarked, "I love that man more than ever." Yes, we have
good reason to be proud of our Colonel, for upon all occasions we
are treated by him as volunteers enlisted in war from pure love
of country, and not regulars, drawn into service from various
other motives, in time of peace.

MAY 16TH.—We rolled out of bed this morning early, and had
our breakfast of slapjacks made of flour, salt and water, which
lie on a man's stomach like cakes of lead—for we are out of all
rations but flour and salt, though we hope soon for some variety.
We heard heavy firing about eleven o'clock. Our division reached
Champion Hill about two P. M., and filed into a field on the right
of the road. We were drawn up in a line facing the woods through
which ran the road we had just left. It was by this road the
rebels came out of Vicksburg to whip us. We had orders to lie
down. The command was obeyed with alacrity, for bullets were
already whizzing over our heads. I never hugged Dixie's soil as
close as I have to-day. We crowded together as tight as we could,
fairly plowing our faces into the ground. Occasionally a ball
would pick its man in spite of precaution, and he would have to

slip to the rear. Soon we got orders to rise up, and in an instant every man was on his feet. If the former order was well obeyed, the latter was equally so. The enemy charged out of the woods in front of us in a solid line, and as they were climbing the fence between us, which separated the open field from the timber, De-Golier's battery, stationed in our front, opened on them with grape and canister, and completely annihilated men and fence, and forced the enemy to fall back. Such terrible execution by a battery 1 never saw. It seemed as if every shell burst just as it reached the fence, and rails and rebs flew into the air together. They, finding our center too strong, renewed their charge on our left, and succeeded in driving it a short distance, but their success was only for a moment, for our boys rallied, and with reinforcements drove them in turn. We now charged into the woods and drove them a little ways, and as we charged over the spot so lately occupied by the foe, we saw the destruction caused by our battery, the ground being covered thickly with rebel grey. When we reached the woods we were exposed to a galling fire, and were at one time nearly surrounded, but we fought there hard until our ammunition was exhausted, when we fixed bayonets and prepared to hold our ground. A fresh supply of ammunition soon came up, when we felt all was well with us again. Meanwhile the right of our line succeeded in getting around to their left, when the enemy retreated towards Vicksburg, lest they should be cut off.

The battle to-day was commenced early in the morning by McClernand's great fighting corps, and was a hot and severe contest, until Logan's division approached the road on the Confederates' left, between them and Vicksburg, when the foe wavered and began to break. This was a hard day's fight, for the rebels, finding that they had been beaten in three battles about Vicksburg, had no doubt resolved to make a desperate stand against our conquering march; but alas! for them, this day's course of events was like the rest. When the fight was over, Generals Grant, McClernand, Sherman, McPherson and Logan rode over the victorious field, greeted with the wildest cheers. I wonder if they love their men as we love them. We received our mail an hour or two after the fight, and the fierce struggle through which we had just passed was forgotten as we read the news from home. Our fingers fresh from the field left powder marks on the white messengers that had come to cheer us.

Crocker, Hovey and Logan's Divisions driving the enemy at the point of the bayonet throught Champion Hills.

Our forces captured eleven pieces of artillery and over one thousand prisoners. The retreating army will make another stand, but we shall move right on, undaunted. Several amusing incidents have occurred during the battle to-day. Company A, of the 20th, was sent out to skirmish, and moved forward till they could see the enemy. By this time General Logan made his appearance, when one of the boys who wished to go into the fight without impediments, approached Logan and said, "General, shall we not unsling knapsacks?" "No," was the stern reply, "damn them, you can whip them with your knapsacks on." This same company, in full view of a rebel battery, had taken refuge in a deep ditch, and when afterward the rebel captain cried out, "ready, take aim," Mit. Bryant, feeling secure in his position, interrupted the order with a shout, "shoot away and be damned to you."

We moved up through the woods to the road again after the fight, where we halted an hour. Near the road was a farm house which was immediately taken possession of for a hospital.

MAY 17TH.—On the road to Vicksburg, resolved to capture the city or get badly whipped. We have not known defeat since we left Fort Donelson, and we propose to keep our good record up. We have seen hard times on some hotly contested fields, but mean to have nothing but victory, if possible, on our banner.

The advance of our army has made a grand sweep, pell-mell, over the rebel works at Big Black River, routing the foe and capturing twenty-five hundred prisoners with twenty-nine cannon. Their rifle pits were quite numerous, but they were all on low ground, so that when the word was given the Yankees rushed over them with the greatest ease. The rebs may be drawing us into a trap, but as yet we have not a moments' fear of the result, for when Grant tells us to go over a thing we go, and feel safe in going. Even in time of peace we would not wish the great curtain that hides the future to be rolled away, nor do soldiers now ask to know what lies before them. But every day brings new scenes fraught with dangers, hair-breadth escapes or death, after which the ranks close and move on undaunted. And our love of country still grows as we go.

We camped within a few miles of Black River, perfectly satisfied, though we have had no hand in the slaughter to-day. We rather expected to be halted a few days at the river, where the enemy would surely be strongly fortified, and where, as they could certainly spare the greater part of their forces from Vicksburg, if they would but bring them out, they could make a desperate stand. We are now fighting hard for our *grub*, since we have nothing left but flour, and slapjacks lie too heavy on a soldier's

Breakfast,	-	Slapjacks.
Dinner,	- -	Slapjacks.
Supper,	-	Slapjacks.

Too many Slapjacks cause a soldier to dream of a feast at home.

stomach. But there is great consolation in reflecting that behind us Uncle Sam keeps piled a bountiful supply all ready to be issued as soon as we can find a proper halting place.

MAY 18TH.—The army last night made pontoons, on which this morning the Black River has been crossed. McClernand is on the left, McPherson in the center, and Sherman on the right. In this position the three great corps will move to Vicksburg by different roads. We are nearing the doomed city, and are now on the lookout for fun.

As we crossed the river and marched up the bank, a brass band stood playing national airs. O, how proud we felt as we marched through the rebel works, and up to the muzzles of the abandoned guns that had been planted to stay our progress. Every man felt the combined Confederate army could not keep us out of Vicksburg. It was a grand sight, the long lines of infantry moving over the pontoons, and winding their way up the bluffs, with flags flying in the breeze, and the morning sun glancing upon the

Sherman's men inflating rubber pontoon on which to cross Big Black River.

guns as they lay across the shoulders of the boys. Cheer after cheer went up in welcome and triumph from the thousands who had already crossed and stood in waiting lines upon the bluff above. This is supposed to be the last halting place before we knock for admittance at our goal—the boasted Gibraltar of the west.

Our division has made a long march to-day, and we have bivouaced for the night without supper, and with no prospect of breakfast, for our rations have been entirely exhausted. Murmurings and complaints are loud and deep, and the swearing fully up to the army standard. General Leggett walked into our camp, and in his usual happy way inquired, "Well, boys, have you had your supper?" "No, General, we have not had any." "Well, boys, I have not had any either, and we shall probably have to fight for our breakfast." "Very well, General; guess we can stand it as well as you," came the ready answer from a score of us, and resignation settled back upon the features of tired and hungry, but unsubdued, patriot soldiers.

"You may study the hopeful, bright brows of these men,
Who have marched all day over hill and throu h glen,
Half clad and unfed; but who is it will dare
Claim to find on those faces one trace of despair?"

MAY 19TH.—This day beholds a cordon of steel, with rivets of brave hearts, surrounding Vicksburg. The enemy left their fortifications on the first, twelfth, fourteenth, sixteenth and eighteenth of this month, and dealt their best blows to prevent the occurrence

of what we have just accomplished—the surrounding of their well
fortified city. We have now come here to compel them to surrender, and we are prepared to do it either by charge or by siege,
and they cannot say to us nay. They have fought well to keep their
homes free from invasion, and surely deserve praise for their
brave return to battle after so many defeats. Our army encircles
the city from the river above to the river below, a distance of
seven and a half miles.

The three corps have taken respective positions as follows:
Sherman's Fifteenth occupies the right of the line, resting on the
river above; General McClernand's Thirteenth touches the river
below, while McPherson's Seventeenth stands in the center. Our
own division, commanded by Logan, occupies the road leading
to Jackson.

In taking our position we did a great deal of skirmishing, and
I suppose the same difficulty was probably experienced by the
rest of the line. We have been nineteen days on the march
around Vicksburg, and the time has been full of excitement—
quite too varied for a comprehensive view just now, but those
who have borne a part in it will store it all away in memory, to
be gone over between comrades by piece-meal, when they meet
after the war is over.

The personal experience of even the humblest soldier will get
a hearing in years to come, for it is the little things in an unusual life that are most entertaining, and personal observations
from the rank and file, narrated by those who saw what they describe, will make some of the most instructive paragraphs of the
war's history.

This has been a day to try the nerves of the boys, while taking
position in front to invest the doomed city. It has been a day to
try men's souls, and hearts, too. The long lines of rebel earth-
works following the zig-zag courses of the hills, and black field
guns still menacing from their port-holes, bristle with defiance
to the invaders.

Our regiment, the 20th Ohio, being ordered in position on
the Jackson road, immediately passed to the left in front of
Fort Hill, where it stood ready to charge at a moment's notice. Meanwhile Colonel Force cautiously made his way in front
of the different companies and spoke familiarly to his men words
of encouragement. Said he, "boys, I expect we shall be ordered
to charge the fort. I shall run right at it, and I hope every man

will follow me." At that instant a soldier of one of the companies on the left was found snugly hid in a ravine under the
roots of a tree, and his lieutenant's attention being called to the
fact, he was ordered out, when he replied, "lieutenant, I do not
believe I am able to make such a charge."

Map of Vicksburg, showing the river front and the positions of the Union and Confederate lines in the rear.

MAY 20TH.—When I awoke this morning I offered thanks to
God that my life had been spared thus far. We slept on our
arms—something unusual. This day has been busily spent in
making cautious advances toward the works of the enemy, and,

although our progress seems to have been very little, we are content to approach step by step, for the task is difficult and dangerous. Bullets are flying over our heads, and it is quite common to see the boys trying to dodge them. A few have succeeded in stopping these bullets, but they had to leave at once for the hospital. A blanket displayed by its owner was called a map of the confederacy, on account of the holes in it made by bullets at Raymond and Champion Hills. It is good enough yet for warmth, but will not do to hold water. We are ragged and dirty, for we have had no change of clothes for over a month. But we have the promise of new suits soon. If we were to enter Vicksburg to-morrow, some of our nice young fellows would feel ashamed to march before the young ladies there. We can see the court house in the city with a confederate flag floating over it. What fun it will be to take that down, and hoist in its stead the old stars and stripes. Then yonder is the Mississippi river again; we want to jump into that once more and have a good bath. The hills back of Vicksburg, and in fact all round the city seem quite steep and barren, and to run in parallels, affording our troops good shelter from batteries and secret approaches. It is upon these hills opposite the town that our tents are pitched. We must cut back into the hills to escape the shower of bullets, for we like to feel secure, when asleep or off duty. A great many of the balls that come over are what are called "spent," that is, have not force enough left to do any harm. We do not feel quite as safe awake or asleep as we did before we got so near the city. However, we manage to sleep pretty much unconcerned as to danger. Our regiment is detailed to watch at the rifle pits in front to-night.

MAY 21ST.—We were relieved this morning before daylight, and slipped back to our camp as quietly as we could. The rifle pits where we watched were pretty close to the enemy, and we had to note every movement made by them. If they put their heads above their works we sent a hundred or more shots at them, and on the other hand, if any on our side made themselves too conspicuous, they fired in turn. So each army is watching the other like eagles. We must be relieved while it is yet dark, for if such a move were attempted by daylight, the enemy could get our range and drop many a man.

The weather is getting very hot, but we do our best to keep cool whether out of battle or in it. It is fortunate for us that our work at the rifle pits occurs at night, when the air is much more cool and pleasant, and the services less fraught with danger. Last night quite a number of new pits were opened and gabions placed on them. Firing from behind these was attended with less danger. Gabions are a sort of wicker-work, resembling round baskets, filled with dirt. The rebel fort in our front was made by cutting away the back half of the hill, leaving the face towards us in a state of nature. This fort is supplied with large guns, but their owners can not use them, as our rifle pits occupy higher ground, from which we watch them too closely.

MAY 22D. —Last night mortar-shells, fired from the boats on the river in front of the city across Point Louisiana, fell thick over all parts of Vicksburg, and at three o'clock this morning every cannon along our line belched its shot at the enemy. Nothing could be heard at the time but the thundering of great guns—one hundred cannons sent crashing into the town —parrot, shrapnell, cannister, grape and solid shot—until it seemed impossible that anything could withstand such a fearful hailstorm. It was indeed a terrible spectacle—awfully grand.

At ten o'clock we had orders to advance. The boys were expecting the order and were busy divesting themselves of watches, rings, pictures

Mortar from the river in front. "During the siege of Vicksburg, sixteen thousand shells were thrown from the mortar gunboats, and naval batteries into the city."—*Hamersly*.

and other keepsakes, which were being placed in the custody of the cooks, who were not expected to go into action. I never saw

such a scene before, nor do I ever want to see it again. The instructions left with the keepsakes were varied. For instance, "This watch I want you to send to my father if I never return"— "I am going to Vicksburg, and if I do not get back just send these little trifles home, will you?"—proper addresses for the sending of the articles being left with them. Not a bit of sadness or fear appears in the talk or faces of the boys, but they thought it timely and proper to dispose of what they had accordingly. This was done while we awaited orders, which at last came in earnest, and in obedience to them we moved up and took our place in the rifle pits within a hundred yards of Fort Hill, where we had orders to keep a diligent watch, and to fire at the first head that dared to show itself. The air was so thick with the smoke of cannon that we could hardly see a hundred yards before us. The line to our right and left was completely hidden from view except as revealed by the flash of guns, and the occasional bursting of shells through the dense clouds. About eleven o'clock came a signal for the entire line to charge upon the works of the enemy. Our boys were all ready, and in an instant leaped forward to find victory or defeat. The seventh Missouri took the lead with ladders which they placed against the fort, and then gave way for others to scale them. Those who climbed to the top of the fort met cold steel, and, when at length it was found impossible to enter the fort that way, the command was given to fall back, which was done under a perfect hail of lead from the enemy. The rebels, in their excitement and haste to fire at our retreating force, thrust their heads a little too high above their cover,—an advantage we were quick to seize with well aimed volleys. In this charge a severe loss was met by our division, and nothing gained. What success was met by the rest of the line I can not say, but I hope it was better than ours. Thus ended another day of bloody fight in vain, except for an increase of the knowledge which has been steadily growing lately, that a regular siege will be required to take Vicksburg. This day will be eventful on the page of history, for its duties have been severe, and many a brave patriot bit the dust under the storm of deadly fire that assailed us.

MAY 23D.—Our regiment lay in the rifle pits to-day, watching the enemy. For hours we were unable to see the motion of a man or beast on their side, all was so exceedingly quiet through-

out the day.   After dark we were relieved, and as we returned to
the camp the enemy got range of us, and for a few minutes their
bullets flew about us quite freely.   However, we bent our

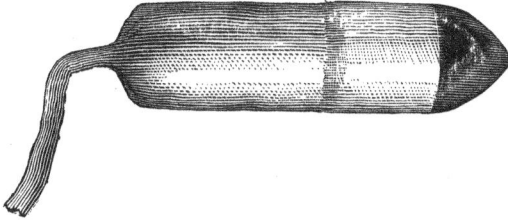

How swift their flight;
What strange wierd music do they make ;
And then, at last,
What curious forms these little minnies take.

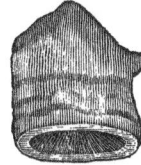

Minnie-balls fired at Vicksburg.

—3

heads as low as we could and double-quicked to quarters. One shot flew very close to my head, and I could distinctly recognize the familiar zip and whiz of quite a number of others at a safer distance. The rebels seemed to fire without any definite direction. If our sharpshooters were not on the alert, the rebels could peep over their works and take good aim; but as they were so closely watched they had to be content with random shooting.

If this siege is to last a month there will be a whole army of trained sharpshooters, for the practice we are getting is making us skilled marksmen. I have gathered quite a collection of balls, which I mean to send home as relics of the siege. They are in a variety of shapes, and were a thousand brought together there could not be found two alike. I have picked up some that fell at my feet—others were taken from trees. I am the only known collector of such souvenirs, and have many odd and rare specimens. Rebel bullets are very common about here now—too much so to be valuable; and as a general thing the boys are quite willing to let them lie where they drop. I think, however, should I survive, I would like to look at them again in after years.

Shovel and pick are more in use to-day, which seems to be a sign that digging is to take the place of charging at the enemy. We think Grant's head is level, anyhow. The weather is getting hotter, and I fear sickness; and water is growing scarce, which is very annoying. If we can but keep well, the future has no fears for us.

MAY 24TH.—Sunday; and how little like the Sabbath day it seems. Cannon are still sending their messengers of death into the enemy's lines, as on week days, and the minnie balls sing the same song, while the shovel throws up as much dirt as on any other day. What a relief it would be if, by common consent, both armies should cease firing to-day. It is our regiment's turn to watch at the front, so before daylight we moved up and took our position. We placed our muskets across the rifle pits, pointing towards the fort, and then lay down and ran our eyes over the gun, with finger on trigger, ready to fire at anything we might see moving. For hours not a movement was seen, till finally an old half-starved mule meandered too close to our lines, when off went a hundred or more muskets, and down fell the poor mule. This little incident, for a few minutes, broke the monotony. A coat and hat were elevated on a stick above our rifle pits, and in an instant they were riddled with bullets from the enemy. The rebels were a little excited at the ruse, and probably thought, after their firing, there must be one less Yankee in our camp. In their eagerness a few of them raised their heads a little above their breastworks, when a hundred bullets flew at them from our side. They all dropped instantly, and we could not tell whether they were hit or not. The rebels, as well as ourselves, occasionally hold up a hat by way of diversion. A shell from an enemy's gun dropped into our camp rather unexpectedly, and bursted near a group, wounding several, but only slightly, though the doctor thinks one of the wounded will not be able to sit down comfortably for a few days. I suppose, then, he can go on picket, or walk around and enjoy the country.

MAY 25TH.—Pemberton sent a flag of truce to Grant at two P. M., and the cessation of hostilities thus agreed on, lasted till eight o'clock in the evening. It made us happy, for we fancied it was a sign they wanted to surrender—but no such good luck. It was simply to give both sides a chance to bury their dead, which had been lying exposed since the twenty-second. Both armies issued from their respective fortifications and pits, and mingled together in various sports, apparently with much enjoyment. Here a group of four played cards—two Yanks and two Rebs. There, others were jumping, while everywhere blue and gray mingled in conversation over the

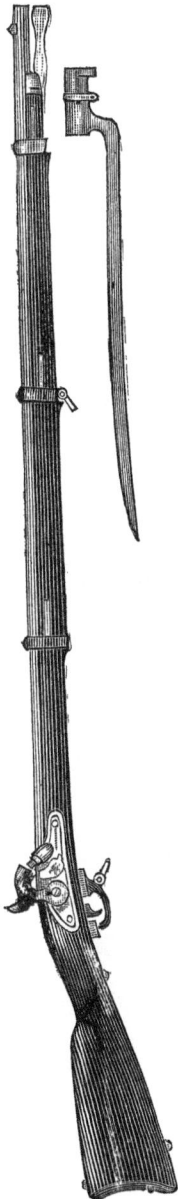

| Vice, | Punch, | Ball-screw, | Screw-driver, | Wiper. |

Rifle-Musket and Appendages.

scenes which had transpired since our visit to the neighborhood.
I talked with a very sensible rebel, who said he was satisfied we
should not only take Vicksburg, but drive the forces of the south
all over their territory, at last compelling them to surrender;

Burying the dead that had lain between the Union and Confederate lines for three days.

still, he said, he had gone into the fight, and was resolved not to back out. He said they had great hope of dissension in the north, to such an extent as might strengthen their cause. There have been grounds for this hope, I am sorry to say, and such dissensions at the north must prolong the war, if our peace party should succeed in materially obstructing the war measures of government. From the remarks of some of the rebels, I judged that their supply of provisions was getting low, and that they had no source from which to draw more. We gave them from our own rations some fat meat, crackers, coffee and so forth, in order to make them as happy as we could. We could see plainly that their officers watched our communications closely.

MAY 26TH.—Up this morning at three o'clock, with orders for three days' rations in our haversacks and five days' in the wagons —also to be ready to move at ten o'clock to the rear, in pursuit of Johnston, who was thrusting his bayonets too close to our boys there.

I am not anxious to get away from the front, yet a little marching in the country will be quite a desirable change, and no doubt beneficial to our men. I have been afraid we might be molested in the rear, for we were having our own way too smoothly to last. I think the confederate authorities are making a great mistake in not massing a powerful army in our rear and thus attempting to break our lines and raise the siege. We shall attend to Johnston, for Grant has planted his line so firmly that he can spare half his men to look out for his rear. What a change we notice to-day, from the time spent around the city, where there was no sound except from the zipping bullets and booming cannon; while out here in the country the birds sing as sweetly as if they had not heard of war at all. Here, too, we get an exchange from the smoky atmosphere around Vicksburg, to heaven's purest breezes.

We have marched to-day over the same ground for which we fought to gain our position near the city. Under these large spreading oaks rest the noble dead who fell so lately for their country. This march has been a surprise to me. It is midnight, and we are still marching.

MAY 27TH.—It was three o'clock this morning before we camped. A tiresome tramp we have had, and after halting, but a few minutes elapsed before we were fast asleep. We were up, however, with the sun, took breakfast and were on the march again at eight o'clock. We halted two hours at noon, during which time we had dinner and rest. Camped again in the evening without having come in contact with the enemy. We do not know where Johnston is, but shall find him if he is in the neighborhood. This excursion party is composed of six regiments, and should we meet Johnston, and his force prove to be the largest, we shall have to fight hard, for we are now some distance from reinforcements. The health of our boys, however, is good—although one of them complains of *worms*—in his crackers. A change from city to country life seems generally acceptable—and yet as it was, our residence was only suburban.

MAY 28TH.—We did not strike out on the war-path again till three P. M. to-day, having spent the time previous in taking a good rest. To-day we have not marched very rapidly, as it has now become necessary to go more slowly in order to feel our way, since we cannot tell what obstacle we may encounter. All the natives we meet along the road claim that Johnston is going to raise the siege. If so, it will prove about the biggest "raising" he ever attended. Camped again about dark.

MAY 29TH.—"The early bird catches the worm." We tried the truth of that adage this morning, but failed to make the catch. A few graybacks were seen afar off, but we failed to get within range of them. Where, O where, is General Johnston and the grand army he was to bring against us? We have looked for him in vain. I have the utmost confidence in Grant's judgment and the prestige of his army which has never yet known defeat, but I confess, till now, I have been afraid of some attack in our rear. And why such a thing does not occur is a mystery to me—at least an attempt at it. Day by day Grant is intrenching and pushing nearer to the enemy's works, planting heavy guns and receiving fresh troops, so the opportunity for a saving stroke by the enemy is fast disappearing.

Camped again at dark, within two miles of Mechanicsville, through which we passed, finding all quiet after our cavalry had driven a few rebs beyond the town.

MAY 30TH.—Moved this morning at four o'clock back again towards Vicksburg—rather an early start, unless some special business awaits us. A few surmise that there is need for us at the front, but I think it is only a freak of General Frank Blair, who is in command of our excursion party. The day has been hot, and we have been rushed forward as though the salvation of the Union depended upon our forced march. I am not a constitutional grumbler, but I fail to understand why we have been trotted through this sultry Yazoo bottom where pure air seems to be a stranger. Probably our commander wants to get us out of it as soon as posible. A few of the men have been oppressed with the heat, and good water is very scarce. This seems to be a very rich soil, made up no doubt of river deposits. A ridge runs parallel with the river, and it is on that elevation all the planta-tion buildings are located, overlooking the rich country around. The Yazoo river is a very sluggish stream and said to be quite deep. The darkies claim it is "dun full of cat-fish." I think we may probably have fresh, fish, but not till we *catch* Vicksburg, and then only in case we are allowed to take a rest, for I presume there will then turn up some other stronghold for Grant and his army to take, and for which we shall have to be off as soon as this job is ended. We camped at dark, after a severe and long march, and it is now raining very hard.

MAY 31ST.—We were aroused by the bugle call, and in a few minutes on the march again. Halted at noon on a large planta-tion. This is a capital place to stop, for the negroes are quite busy baking corn-bread and sweet potatoes for us. We have had a grand dinner at the expense of a rich planter now serving in the southern army. Some of the negroes wanted to come with us, but we persuaded them to remain, telling them they would see hard times if they followed us. They showed indications of good treatment, and I presume their master is one of the few who treat their slaves like human beings.

I must say—whether right or wrong—plantation life has had a sort of fascination for me ever since I came south, especially when I visit one like that where we took dinner to-day, and some, also, I visited in Tennessee. I know I should treat my slaves well, and, while giving them a good living, I should buy, but never sell.

We left at three o'clock P. M., and just as the boys were ordered to take with them some of the mules working in the field, where there was a large crop being cultivated, to be used, when gathered, for the maintenance of our enemies. As our boys, accordingly, were unhitching the mules, some "dutchy" in an officer's uniform rode up, yelling, "mens! you left dem schackasses alone!" I doubt whether he had authority to give such an order, but whether he had or not he was not obeyed. When we marched off with our corn-bread and "schackasses," some of the darkies insisted on following. We passed through some rebel works at Haines' Bluffs, which were built to protect the approach to Vicksburg by way of the Yazoo river. Sherman had taken them on the nineteenth instant, when our boats came up the river and delivered rations.

May has now passed, with all its hardships and privations to the army of the west—the absence of camp comforts; open fields for dwelling places; the bare ground for beds; cartridge boxes for pillows, and all the other tribulations of an active campaign. Enduring these troubles, we have given our country willing service. We have passed through some hard-fought battles, where many of our comrades fell, now suffering in hospitals or sleeping, perhaps, in unmarked graves. Well they did their part, and much do we miss them. Their noble deeds shall still incite our emulation, that their proud record may not be sullied by any act of ours.

Camped at dark, tired, dirty and ragged—having had no chance to draw clothes for two months.

JUNE 1ST.—We stayed in camp all day, much to the enjoyment of the boys. Sergeant Hoover and I got a horse and mule, and rode down to Chickasaw Bayou, where the supplies for our army around Vicksburg are received. I have complained a little of being overmarched, but the trotting of my mule to-day was the hardest exercise I have had for some time.

If our poor foes in Vicksburg could see our piles of provisions on the river landing, they might hunger for defeat. Around Vicksburg the country is quite hilly and broken, with narrow ridges, between which are deep ravines. These ridges are occupied by the opposing forces at irregular distances. At some points the lines of the Union and Confederate armies are but fifty yards apart.

JUNE 2D.—We stayed in camp again all day, and I improved the time strolling through the camps, forts and rifle pits, which

Receiving supplies at Chickasaw Bayou for the army around Vicksburg.

had been deserted by the Confederates. They seem to have left their quarters rather unceremoniously, for they abandoned siege guns, with tents, wagons, clothing and ammunition scattered about in confusion. I thought, while camped here, they seemed to feel quite secure. They frequently looked towards the Yazoo, and defied our boats to come up. However, when the boats did come, with Sherman in the rear, they beat a hasty retreat to the inside of Vicksburg.

As our duties have been light to-day, the time has been occupied socially, by the boys reciting many little scenes of the past month. We conversed feelingly of those left behind on acount of sickness, or wounds, or death in battle. Only half our company is left now, and after two years more, what will have become of the rest? We shall fight on, perhaps, till the other half is gone. The friendship that now exists among our remnant is very firmly knit. Through our past two years of soldier life such ties of brotherhood have grown up as only companions in arms can know. And I trust before the end of another two years the old flag will again float secure in every State in the Nation.

JUNE 3D.—Expected to move to-day, but got orders instead to remain in camp. Have heard heavy cannonading towards Vicksburg. Would prefer to take our place in the line around the city rather than stay away, for there is glory in action. It may be very nice, occasionally, to rest in camp, but to hear firing and to snuff the battle afar off, creates a natural uneasiness. Besides, if the city should surrender in the meantime, we might be

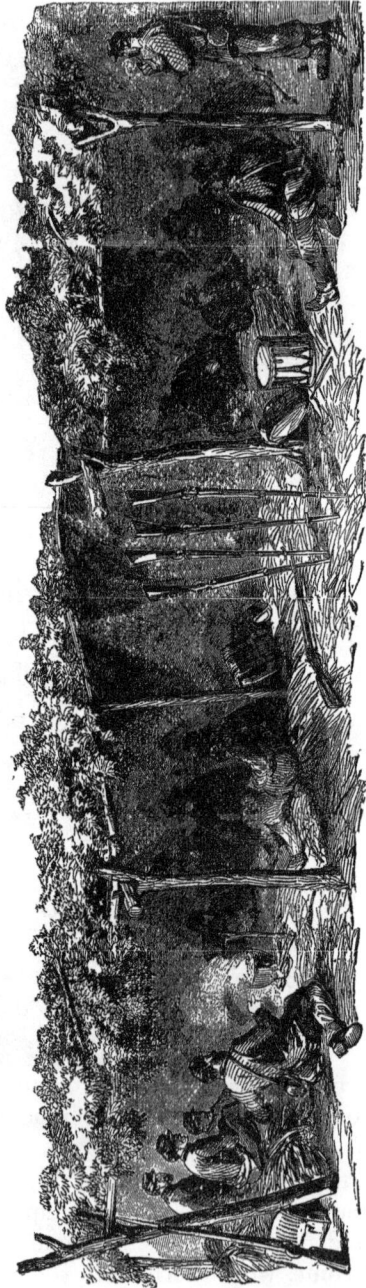

The Bright Side of Siege Life—Camping in the Rear.

cheated out of our share in a prize, to the taking of which we have contributed some valuable assistance.

Newsboys are thick in camp, with the familiar cries, "Chicago Times" and "Cincinnati Commercial." The papers sell quite freely. At home each man wants to buy a paper for himself, but here a single copy does for a whole company, and the one that buys it reads it aloud— a plan which suits the buyer very well, if not the seller. While some of these papers applaud the bravery of the generals and their commands, and pray that the brilliancy of past achievements be not dimmed by dissensions in the face of the enemy, other papers have articles that sound to us like treason, slandering the soldier and denouncing the government. But they can not discourage or demoralize this army, for it was never stronger or more determined than now, and it will continue to strike for our country, even though bleeding at every pore. The rebels can not be subdued, so they say. Why not? In two years have we not penetrated to the very center of the South? And in less than that time we shall be seen coming out, covered all over with victory, from the other side.

June 4th.—We move at last. We left camp as the sun rose, reaching our old quarters in front of the rebel Fort Hill in the afternoon. Glad we are to get here. A great change has taken place during our ten days' absence. More rifle-pits have been made and new batteries erected, and our lines generally have been pushed closer to the works of the enemy. Mines are being dug, and we shall soon see something flying in the air in front of us, when those mines explode. The work is being done very secretly, for it would not do to have the rebels find out our plans. Fort Hill in our front and on the Jackson road is said to be the key to Vicksburg. We have tried often to turn this key, but have as often failed. In fact, the lock is not an easy one. The underground work now going on will perhaps break the lock with an explosion. Our return to camp from our excursion after Johnston creates some excitement among those who stayed behind. They all want to hear about our trip, and what we saw and conquered. Our clothes are so dirty and ragged, that though we have sewed and patched, and patched and sewed, Uncle Sam would hardly recognize those nice blue suits he gave us a little while ago. This southern sun pours down a powerful heat, which compels us to keep as quiet as possible. Just a month from to-day we celebrate our Fourth of July—where, I do not know, but inside of Vicksburg, I hope.

I have asked both officers and men to write in an album I have opened since reaching our old post near the city, and here are a few of their contributions:

"*Friend O.:* Here is hoping we may see the stars and stripes float over the court house in Vicksburg on the Fourth of July, and also that we may see this rebellion, in which so many of our comrades have fallen, come to an end, while we live on to enjoy a peace secured by our arms. Then hurrah for the Buckeye girls. Your sincere friend,

"Henry H. Fulton,
" Company E, 20th Ohio."

" Here is hoping we may have the pleasure of *zweiglass* of lager in Vicksburg, on July 4th.

" D. M. Cooper,
" Company A, 96th Ohio."

" I hope we shall be able to spend the coming Fourth in the famous city before us, and to have a glorification there over our victories.

" Squire McKee,
" Company E, 20th Ohio."

" Here is hoping that by the glorious Fourth, and by the force of our arms, we shall penetrate their boasted Gibraltar.

"T. B. LEGGETT,
" Company E, 20th Ohio."

" I offer you this toast: Though you have seen many hardships, let me congratulate you on arriving safely so near Vicksburg. May the besieged city fall in time for you and all our boys to take a glass of lager on the Fourth of July; and may the boys of the Twentieth be the first to taste the article they have duly won.

"D. B. LINSTEAD,
" Company G, 20th Ohio."

JUNE 5TH.—The siege is still progressing favorably. There is joy in our camp, for Uncle Sam has again opened a clothing store, which we shall patronize, asking nothing about price or quality. The boys cheered lustily when they saw the teams drive in, and heard what they were loaded with. However, I don't want to hug rifle-pits with a brand new suit on, for it would soon get dirty.

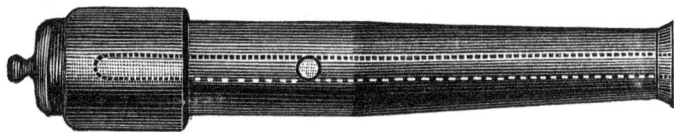

Parrott Rifle.

JUNE 6TH.—Still banging away. I took a horseback ride around the line to the left in the rear of McClernand's corps. Everywhere I went I was met with the familiar zip, zip, of rebel bullets flying promiscuously through the air. I read a northern rebel paper, received by a member of the 96th Ohio, filled with false statements about the soldiers around Vicksburg. It said a great many of Grant's soldiers were deserting. This is of course false, for I have heard of but two deserting their flag in time of need. Those two will never be able to look their old comrades in the face, for if they escape the penalty of death, disgrace and ignominy will not only follow them through life, but stamp their memories and lineage with infamy. The scorn of every loyal soldier will follow these cowards who have deserted in the face of the foe. No true-hearted mother or father can welcome the return of such recreants, who not only disgrace themselves but all their kindred. This paper also stated that the soldiers around Vicksburg are dying off like flies. This is another falsehood, for the army is in good health and spirits, and looking forward to victory with assurance.

JUNE 7TH.—The 20th was at the front all day, sharp shooting. There is a good deal of danger in this kind of business, but we have our fun at it notwithstanding. Another effigy hoisted a little above our rifle-pits, in an instant drew the fire of the enemy. It was our ruse to get them to raise their heads a little, and when they did, we fired back, and the result generally justified the refrain to which our thoughts were moving,

> Should a rebel show his pate,
> To withdraw he'll prove too late.

We have caught them that way several times.

We still keep unshaken confidence in General Grant, and the ultimate success of our cause. We shall stand firm at our posts, yielding cheerful obedience to all orders, and march bravely on without halting to wrangle and grumble at every imaginary short-coming in our officers, while our country is in such distress, and when her cries are borne to us upon every breeze. To be in Grant's army, McPherson's corps, Logan's division and the 20th Ohio, commanded by our brave and courteous colonel, M. F. Force, is to be as well off as any soldier in any army in the world.

JUNE 8TH.—Another day born in the midst of the rattle of shot and shell. Each day finds us more firmly entrenched amid these hills, until we begin to feel ourselves impregnable.

I visited one of the teeming hospitals to see some boys, and it made me sad enough to look upon some who will soon pass from these scenes of strife. One smooth-cheeked little artillery lad closed his eyes forever, with a last lingering look upon the flag he had hoped to see waving over Vicksburg. His last look was at the flag—his last word was "mother!" Poor boy, when he left home he knew little of the hardships and privations to be endured. War is quite another thing from what my schooldays pictured it. I used to think the two contending armies would march face to face and fire at each other, column by column, but experience has shown me a very different picture, for when the command to fire is given it is often when each man must fire at will, taking shelter where he can, without going too far from his line.

Digging a mine under Fort Hill, with a cotton car as protection from the enemy's bullets.

JUNE 9TH.—To-day our regiment was at the front. The rebels kept pretty quiet; they are learning to behave very well. In fact they might as well lie low and save their powder.

Our men have been employed digging a ditch leading up to Fort Hill, when they intend tunneling and blowing up the fort. The rebels, however, have got range of the men digging, and have fired upon them. The answering Yankee trick was to shove a car of cotton bales over the trench toward the fort, while the men worked behind it. This served a good purpose for awhile, till the rebs managed to set it on fire; not to be out-done, our boys pushed forward another car well soaked with water. Another Yankee device was contrived—a tower, ten or twelve feet high, with steps inside running to the top, where was hung a looking-glass in such a position as to catch and reflect, to a man inside the tower, the interior of the enemy's fort and rifle pits, and thus every man and gun could be counted. This latter contrivance,

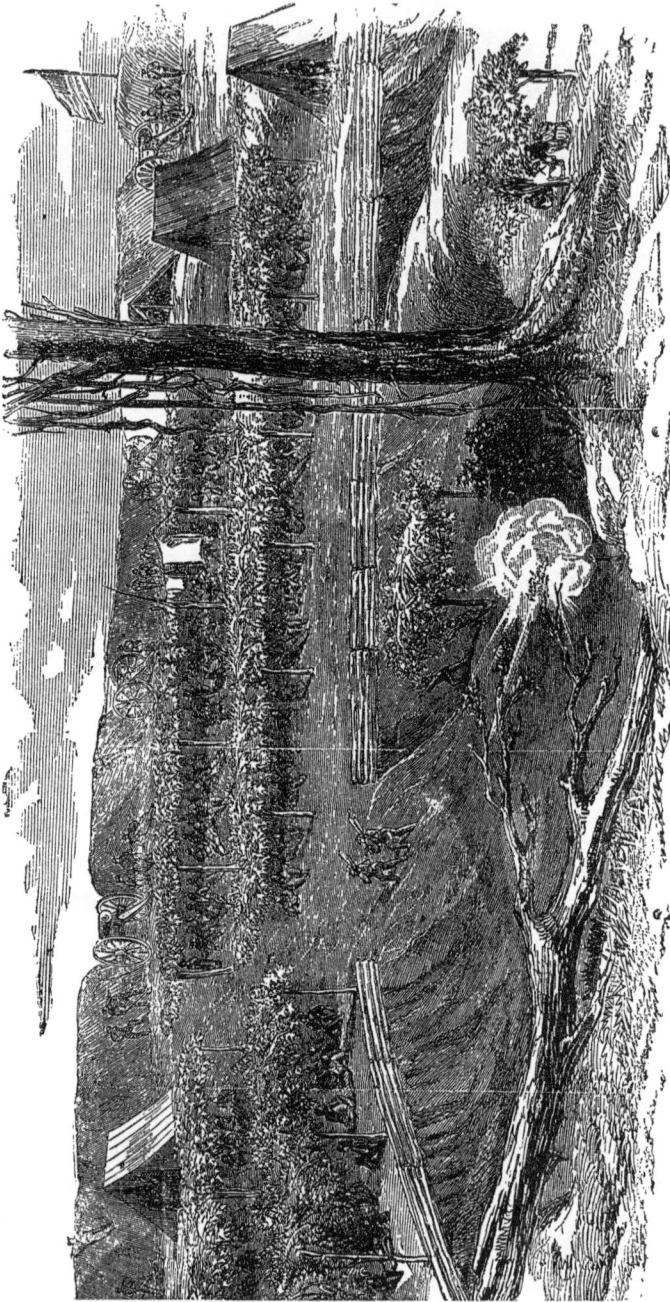

Sheltered from the sun, but not the enemy's shells.

however, did not last long; it became too conspicuous and dangerous for use.

A report creeps into camp that Johnston is coming with fifty thousand men to raise the siege, but I do not believe it. We have often heard that Richmond had fallen, but it continues within the confederate lines. If the army of the Potomac does not soon take it, Grant will march us there and seize the prize from them.

The Yankee Lookout.

JUNE 10TH.—The heat of the sun increases, and we must improve our quarters. Accordingly a part of the day has been spent in cutting cane and building bunks with it on the side of the hill. Such improvements protect us better from the sun.

Last night I sat on the top of a hill awhile, watching the mortar shells flying into the city from the river. High into the air they leaped, and, like falling stars, dropped, exploding among the houses and shaking even the very hills. The lighted fuse of each shell could be seen as it went up and came down, and occasionally I have seen as many as three of them in the air at once. The fuse is so gauged as to explode the shell within a few feet of the ground. The destruction being thus wrought in the city must be very great. We learn from prisoners that the inhabitants are now living in caves dug out of the sides of the hills. Alas! for the women, children and aged in the city, for they must suffer, indeed, and, should the siege continue several months, many deaths from sickness as well as from our shells, must occur. I am sure Grant has given Pemberton a chance to remove from Vicksburg all who could not be expected to take part in the fearful struggle.

We have been looking for rain to cool the air and lay the dust, and this afternoon we were gratified by a heavy shower.

JUNE 11TH.—Stayed in camp to-day with the exception of about an hour. The rebs have succeeded in planting a mortar, which has sent a few big shells into our quarters. This sort of practice did not last long, for a hundred guns around our line soon roared the mortar to silence. But one shell dropped near my tent,

—4

buried itself in the earth, and exploded, scattering dirt for yards around and leaving a hole big enough to bury a horse. Another fell on top of the hill and rolled down, crashing through a tent. The occupants not being at home it failed to find a welcome.

Sibley Tent.

These shells are visitors we do not care to see in camp, for their movements are so clumsy they are apt to break things as they go. However, they are rather rare, while the bullets are so frequent that we have almost ceased to notice them. Their flights remind us of the dropping of leaves and twigs from the trees around us. The balls of lead as they fall are found bent and flattened in every conceivable shape. A friend from the 96th Ohio, on a visit to me, as he walked over, met a rebel bullet which took a piece out of his arm.

JUNE 12TH.—We expect to be paid off soon, as the pay-rolls are now being made out. Money cannot do us much good here among the hills, but we can send it home. Many a family is dependent upon the thirteen dollars a month drawn here by the head of it.

When the war is over, how many soldiers will be unable to earn even their own living, to say nothing of that of their families, all on account of wounds or disability incurred in the service. I have heard many a one say he would rather be shot dead in a fight than lose a limb, and thus be compelled to totter through life disabled. But I know our country will be too magnanimous to neglect its brave defenders who have fought its battles till they have become incapacitated for further service. I know we are not fighting for a country that will let its soldiers beg for a living.

We have now but a year left of the term of our enlistment, and the boys are already talking about what they will do. Some say they will stay till peace comes, no matter how long may be the delay, and I think the majority are of this mind. A few, however, will seek their homes when their time runs out, should this war last so long, and the Lord and rebel bullets spare them. For myself, I shall stay, if I can, till the stars and stripes float in triumph once more over all the land.

Here are a few lines:

TO COMPANY E.

You started at your country's call
    To tread the fields of blood and strife,
Consenting to give up your all—
    All, even to your very life.
And many storms of leaden rain
    And iron hail have been your lot;
While yet among the number slain
    The dear ones North have read you not.

Oh, may you safely yet return
    To those who wait your coming, too;
May their fond hearts not vainly yearn
    To greet you when the war is through.
But, though I wish you back in peace,
    'Tis not a peace that quite *disarms*—
'Tis not a full and sure release,
    You simply take up *other arms*.

JUNE 13TH.—The siege continues with increased fury, and the boom of cannon announces the sacrifice of more lives. Instead of any cessation the artillery plays upon the city almost every moment throughout the day. The variety of the projectiles becomes greater. The shrapnel, I think, must be most formidable

SHRAPNEL.—Containing 80 musket balls, fired at Vicksburg. The conception of this missile is due to Lieut. Gen'l Henry Shrapnel, of the English army. Its velocity is about 1,000 feet per second.

to the enemy. It is a shell filled with eighty small balls, which, when the shell is exploded, scatter in every direction. It makes a fearful buzzing sound as it flies—a warning to seek cover, if such can be found. Besides this there are the parrot, cannister, grape

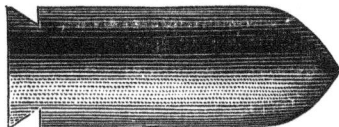

Parrot rifle projectile.

and solid shot. The cannister and grape are also cases wherein are enclosed a number of small balls. But the least fragment from an exploded shell is sufficient to wound or kill.

I have a great curiosity to see the court house at Vicksburg. It stands on a hill, and seems to be the target for many cannon.

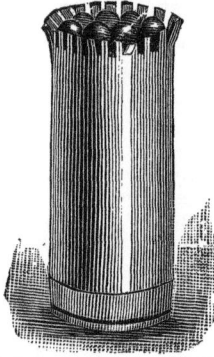

There is a Confederate flag waving from it defiantly. A proud day it will be when we haul it down and raise in its stead the stars and stripes, never to be displaced again. The buildings in the city must, by this time, be pretty well riddled with shot and shell. The women, it seems, did not all leave the city before the bombardment began, and I suppose they have determined to brave it out. Their sacrifices and privations are worthy of a better cause, and were they but on our side how we would worship them.

Cannister shot is a tin cylinder with iron heads, filled with balls packed with saw-dust. The heads are movable, and the edges of the tin are turned down over them to hold them in place. The balls are made of such a size that seven of them can lie in a bed, one in the middle and six around. These balls are made of cast iron, and are 28 in number.

Grape Shot.

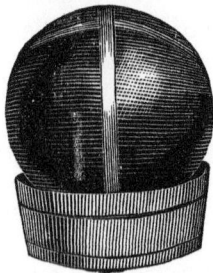

Solid Shot strapped on a Sabot.

It is rumored in camp that Grant is getting reinforcements from the eastern army. I have a great desire to see them, for while we have always thought them to be no less brave, they are said to be better clothed and equipped than the western boys. In fact, from the eastern army, during the last year, the standing report among western boys has been merely such catch phrases as "Bull Run," "Burnside Crossing the Rappahannock," "All Quiet on the Potomac." Perhaps such reports or their substance will continue to fill the headlines of news from those departments until Lincoln commissions Grant commander of the whole army. Should that occur, one grand move forward will be made and the Southern confederacy will be crushed forever.

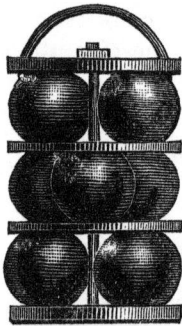

We are doing all we can to expedite the glorious victory awaiting us here, yet there are grumblers in the North who are complaining of our slow progress, and treasonable articles are published in some papers that come to us from the North, intended to discourage the soldiers. Why don't Grant move? If we had all those grumblers in Vicksburg, I fancy they would soon find something from Grant was moving quite briskly. But Grant does not idle away his time himself, nor let his men be idle. If the people of the North will but back us up with their aid and confidence, we shall feel well repaid for all the sufferings we endure here, staring death in the face, and standing like a solid wall between their homes and danger.

Let not a murmur meet the ear,
Nor discontent have sway;
Let not a sullen brow appear
Through all the camp to-day.

JUNE 14TH.—Sunday. No bells to ring us to church. I wish we had one day in seven for rest and freedom from care; but there is no such thing now for the soldier. It is shoot, shoot, dodge, dodge, from morning to night, without cessation, except when we are asleep. When the time comes, we can lie down and sleep soundly all night, right under our cannon, firing over us all the time, without disturbing us in the least. But let the long roll be sounded—every man is up at the first tap—for that sound we know means business for us.

Occasionally the rebs plant a mortar in some out of the way spot and drop a shell or two into our midst; but a few well directed shots from our big guns at the rear soon settle them. These rebels obey very well.

We have several large siege guns, lately planted in the rear of our division, which it took ten yoke of oxen to haul, one at a time, to their places. I had been told that the balls from these guns could be seen on their journey, and could not believe it until I put myself in range of the monsters, just behind them, when I found I could see the balls distinctly, as they flew across the hills towards Vicksburg. These guns are nine-inch calibre and they are about twelve feet long. They are monsters, and their voices are very loud.

Sunday is general inspection day, and the officers passed through our quarters at 10 A. M., finding our guns and accoutrements bright and clean. If any young lady at the North needs a good housekeeper, she can easily be accommodated by making a requisition on the 20th Ohio. In fact we can all do patchwork, sew on buttons, make beds and sweep; but I do not think many of us will follow the business after the war is done, for the "relief" always so anxiously looked for by the soldiers must then come.

I heard one of our boys—a high private in the rear rank—lament that he was

> "Only a private, and who will care
> When I shall pass away?"

Poor lad, he was in a sad way! But it was mere homesickness that ailed him. If dissatisfied with his position as a private, let him wait, for if he survives the war, he will, no doubt, have a chance to be captain of an *infant-ry* company.

JUNE 15TH.—Our regiment went into the rifle-pits again before daylight, at which time the din of musketry and cannonading from both sides had begun, and will cease only when darkness covers the earth.

We are now so close to Fort Hill that a hard tack was tossed into it by one of our boys, and then held up on a bayonet there, to satisfy us of its safe arrival. Some of the boys have become reckless about the rifle-pits, and are frequently hit by rebel bullets. Familiarity breeds a contempt of danger.

Some of the boys wounded at Raymond have got back to us, and are now ready again to do their part. They are, however, more timid than we who have been at the front so long. It is fun to see these new-comers dodge the balls as they zip along. But they, too, will soon become accustomed to flying lead.

Several of the boys have been hit, but not hurt badly, as the balls were pretty nearly spent before reaching them. Those returning from Raymond say they have marked the graves there, but I fear it will not be long before the last vestige of the resting places of our late comrades will be lost.

JUNE 16TH.—We were relieved before daylight, and returned to camp pretty tired. I did not feel well last night, and having had no chance to sleep, I am a little the worse for wear this morning.

There was not much firing done during the night, but we had to keep a good lookout, as there are apprehensions of an outbreak. I do not often go star-gazing, but last night I sat and watched the beauty above. Daytime is glorious, but when night unfurls her banner over care-worn thousands among these hills, and the stars come out from their hiding places, our thoughts seek loftier levels. It was just as though one day had died, and another was born to take its place. Not a breeze stirred the foliage, except as fanned by the whirling shells. My thoughts were of home, and of the dear sister there, bedridden, with but little hope of health again. Her dearest wish, I know, is to see her only brother once more before she passes away to that heavenly peace for which she is destined. Through these terrible two years past, thoughts of home and a safe return to an unbroken family circle, have been my constant guiding star.

*SCHENKLE'S PROJECTILE.

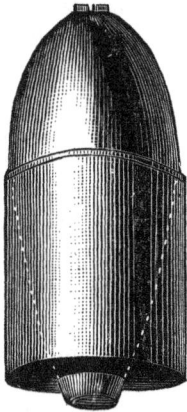 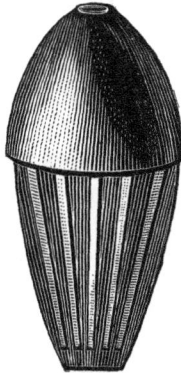

No. 1.   No. 2.

JUNE 17TH.—I was detailed to the charge of a squad of men to guard rebel prisoners in the corral at Logan's headquarters. They were not hard to guard, for they think themselves in pretty good hands, and surely they seem to get better grub here than in their own lines. Some of them are deserters, and upon such I look with contempt. I am ready to share my rations with an honest prisoner, but have no use for a man who enlists in a cause, and then deserts his comrades when they get into a tight place.

If what they say is true, the garrison over there is already familiar with mule meat and scanty meal rations. If they have had to eat mules such as we have killed in the trenches, I pity them, for they are on a tough job. Several cows which I suppose had served families there with milk, we had to kill for browsing too close to our lines.

*This projectile, as shown in No. 1, is composed of a cast-iron body. The expanding portion is a papier-mache wad, which being forced on to the cone. is expanded into the rifling of the bore. On issuing from the bore, the wad is blown to pieces. leaving the projectile entirely unincumbered in its flight through the air (No. 2.)

I am pretty well convinced Pemberton would not hold out much longer but for the help he expects from Johnston. If that, however, is all the hope they have, they might as well surrender at once, for if Johnston should come, he can not do them any good.

A ball struck a little drummer boy a while ago, and he limped off, whimpering: "I wouldn't care a darn, but my other leg has been shot already." Some of the boys went to his assistance, and then they had to hurry towards the hospital, for the rebels got range of them and began firing quite briskly.

I was quite amused to see one of the prisoners brought in to-day, eating his supper. We gave him all he could eat, and that was no small amount. But he was certainly a very hungry man, and if he is a fair sample of those remaining in Vicksburg, Uncle Sam's commissary will have to endure quite a burden, for after the surrender, no doubt, Grant will have to feed them all.

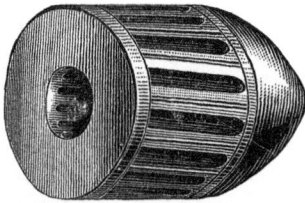

James shell, before the application of the packing.

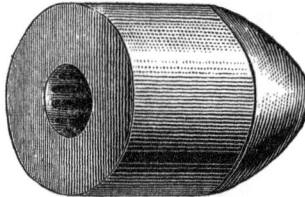

James shell, after the application of the packing, ready for use.

JUNE 18TH.—I was relieved from guard at 9 A. M. and returned to camp. There has been very heavy firing all day, and it is rumored that Pemberton will try to break through our lines; but if he tries that game he will find it dangerous enough. It is no easy matter to climb over the bulwark of steel now encircling this city.

The weather is getting altogether too hot for comfort. A few sun-strokes have occurred, but without proving fatal so far. One poor fellow even dropped at midnight, when I presume the surgeon's diagnosis must have been—moonstruck. There are more ways than one of shirking a battle, for which purpose some are even willing to part with a finger or toe.

If the rebels are short of provisions, their ammunition seems to hold out, for they are quite liberal in their distribution of it. But when Sherman begins firing from the east, McClernand from the west, McPherson from the rear, and the mortars from the north, then look out for big fire-works. The

Aiming at the Court House.

cannon are all pointed towards the town, but some of the shells fall far short of it. When these burst in mid-air, we can see a small round cloud of smoke left behind, and then there is a sharp

A game of euchre, with a shell for trumps.

lookout for fragments to be scattered in every direction. Our artillerymen have had such good practice during the siege, that they can generally drop a shell wherever they want to.

Boys at the front have time for sport, which is not to be interrupted even by stray shells. I noticed four of our boys playing euchre, when a shell from the enemy came careering just above their heads; but they treated it with entire indifference. Another group I saw playing "seven-up" under a blanket caught at the four corners in the hammers of muskets stuck in the ground, and thereby forming a very good shelter from the sun. A shell burst right over this group, scattering its fragments all around, but even this failed to disturb the game, further than to call forth the timely comment, "Johnny passes."

JUNE 19TH.—For a month we have been watching our enemy vigilantly, and a panorama, consisting of a great variety of war scenes, has, during that time, passed before us. We have had charging, digging rifle-pits, blowing up forts and firing all sizes of cannon, to say nothing of percussion shells, spherical case shot, time shells, parrot, grape, cannister, shrapnel, etc., the memory of which will be vivid to all, both blue and gray, who have seen the show around Vicksburg.

Whitworth Projectile.

The terrible noises, too, that have rung in our ears, must echo for years to come. I may add our endurance of this southern sun, at times being short of rations, and at no time out of danger, yet all the time nearly uncomplaining—every one trying to make the best of it, and all as merry as the situation would admit. Each day some of the boys have come in relating new discoveries on reconnoisance, and I do not think there is a foot of ground about these hills that has not been explored, a well or spring that has not been tested, or a single object of interest of any kind that has not been worked till it grew stale. Then each man has had his peculiar view of how a siege like this ought

SHELL WITH FUSE.—The fuse is graduated on the outside into equal parts, representing seconds and quarter-seconds. In the bottom of this channel is a smooth layer of a composition of lead and tin, with a piece of wick or yarn underneath it. On this is placed a piece of metal. When ready for firing, the dial is gauged at the proper point at which the fuse is to burn through into the shell.

to be conducted—that is, from the standpoint of rank and file.

However, we are all agreed that the quiet man in command of our forces is still able to anticipate the requirements of our situation. I call him quiet, for that is just what he is. There is no dash or glitter about him, but he is marked by a steady nerve, and piercing glance that seems to be always on the alert. Many a second lieutenant has fallen a victim to the sharpshooter because of his fresh uniform, while officers of more experience have escaped under slouched hats and old blouses. There seems to be no limit, however, to the experience of some of them.

A cook of the 96th Ohio happened to be cooking beans the other day, when Gen. A. J. Smith, commanding a division of the 13th Army Corps, came around on camp inspection. After being properly saluted by the cook, the general began a colloquy as follows:

Gen. Smith.—What are you cooking?

The Cook.—Beans, sir.

General Smith.—How long do you cook beans?

The Cook.—Four hours, sir.

Gen. Smith (with a look of withering scorn).—*Four hours! You cook 'em six hours!*

That cook's beans were tender enough that day.

"Once again the fire of hell
Rained the rebel quarters,
With scream of shot and burst of shell,
And bellowing of the mortars."

Hand-grenade thrown from Fort Hill.

JUNE 20TH.—This morning our whole line of artillery—seven miles long—opened on the doomed city and fortifications at six o'clock, and kept up the firing for four hours, during which time the smoke was so thick we could see nothing but the flash of the guns. No fog could have so completely hid from view objects around, both close and familiar. Had the rebs made a dash for liberty then, they could not have been discovered until they were right upon us. But they did not do it. Our infantry was all called out in line of battle, and we stacked arms till the firing ceased. O, what a calm after that terrific bellowing. There was every variety of tone to-day from the dogs of war—from the squeak of a little fiste to the roar of a bull dog. The sound of some brass pieces was so loud as to drown the reverberations of the larger guns, and not a return shot was fired.

Fighting over the enemy's fortifications.

Poor fellows, how tamely they took it! They had nothing to say—at least that we could hear. Several of our boys laid down and slept during the firing as soundly as if they had been on their mothers' feather beds at home. When the clouds cleared away I thought the stars and stripes never looked so beautiful. Even if the defenceless women and children in Vicksburg are protected, or feel as if they were, such a screeching of shot and shell must prove a terror to them, and my heart has not yet grown so hardened that I can not feel for them.

There is a good deal of complaint, in our company at least, about the coffee we get. It seems not quite so good as that we have had, and I suspect it has been adulterated by somebody who is willing to get rich at the expense of the poor soldier, whose curses will be heaped strong and heavy on anybody who deteriorates any of his rations, and particularly his coffee. The only time a soldier can not drink his coffee is when the use of that ration is suspended. In fact, there is nothing so refreshing as a cup of hot coffee, and no sooner has a marching column halted, than out from each haversack comes a little paper sack of ground coffee, and a tin cup or tin can, with a wire bale, to be filled from the canteen and set upon a fire to boil. The coffee should not be put in the water before it boils. At first I was green enough to do so, but soon learned better, being compelled to march before the water boiled, and consequently lost my coffee. I lost both the water and the coffee. It takes but about five minutes to boil a cup of water, and then if you have to march you can put your coffee in and carry it till it is cool enough to sip as you go. Even if we halt a dozen times a day, that many times will a soldier make and drink his coffee, for when the commissary is full and plenty, we may drink coffee and nibble crackers from morning till night. The aroma of the first cup of coffee soon sets the whole army to boiling; and the best vessel in which to boil coffee for a soldier is a common cove oyster can, with a bit of bent wire for a bale, by which you can hold it on a stick over the fire, and thus avoid its tipping over by the burning away of its supports.

June 21st.—To-day again church bells at the North are calling good people to worship, and to hear words of cheer and comfort to the soul. The prayers of our patriotic mothers and fathers that will go up to-day for the suppression of this rebellion will surely have a hearing.

We had inspection of arms and quarters at nine this morning. Of course everything was in good order, but if such a thing should take us by surprise some time, our beds might be found not made, and things in general upside down. When notice of this inspection was given, or rather an order to prepare for it, one of our boys remarked, "This must be Sunday;" and he added, "I guess I won't wait for this inspection,—I'll take my girl to church." If his girl had been here the whole company would doubtless have wanted to go to church, too. "Though lost to sight, to memory dear." We can talk to the sweet creatures only through the dear letters exchanged; but a love letter brings a very bright smile to a warrior's face, and the sunshine that prevails in camp after the reading of the mail from home, is quite noticeable. Dear girls, do not stop writing; write letters that are still longer, for they are the sweetest of war's amenities, and are the only medicine that has kept life in the veins of many a homesick soldier. When the mail comes I cannot help wishing everybody may get a letter; but alas! some must miss hearing their names read, and oh! the sadness that creeps over them when the last name has been called and the last letter handed out to some one else. They are sadder than if wounded by a bullet. If wounded, a surgeon may prescribe; but what prescription for the failure of a letter from home? Our mail is by no means daily, and if it comes at all, its favors are few and far between. Indeed, each time it comes we get to feeling as if it may never come again. And so it may prove, in fact. The disappointed one carries his strangled hope into the next day's fight, falls, and dies, perhaps, from some wound that otherwise might prove slight, for his heart is broken.

This afternoon I stood on a little hill just back of a regiment adjoining, talking with a friend there, when crash through his brain went a rebel bullet. He had just alluded to the horrors of the daily strife. Relieved from further duty here, he went to answer roll-call in a better army, to which his honorable discharge from this ought surely to admit him. He answered the first call of his country, and had served faithfully through two years of hardship and danger. I personally know that he fought well, and his name should not fail to be enrolled somewhere in the records of his country.

JUNE 22D.—Johnston is getting lively again, and beginning to kick up a dust in the rear; so we have orders to move to-night, with three days' cooked rations. One regiment from each brigade in Logan's division constitute our expedition, which, I think, will find him, and if we get sight of his army, somebody will be likely to get hurt.

It is now just a month since we made the charge on the enemy's line which proved to us so disastrous, and our cannon now are too close to act on Fort Hill, so a wooden gun has been made, which, charged with a small amount of powder, throws the shell inside the fort—a new device, but working well, for it can drop its missile where the cannon cannot.

We have eaten pretty well in camp to-day, and cooked everything we had on hand, since we may not get so good an opportunity again upon the march. When hard tack was first issued there was but one way to eat it, and that was dry, just as it reached us. Practice, however, taught us to prepare a variety of dishes from it. The most palatable way to dispose of hard tack, to my taste, is to pulverize, then soak over night, and fry for breakfast as batter-cakes. Another good way is to soak whole, and then fry; and still another is to soak a little, then lay it by the fire and let grease drop on it from toasted meat, held to the fire on a pointed stick. This latter is the most common way on a march. Sometimes the tack is very hard indeed by the time it reaches us, and it requires some knack to break it. I have frequently seen boys break it over their knees. Just raise your foot up so as to bring the bent knee handy, and then fetch your hard tack down on it with your right hand, with all the force you can spare, and, if not too tough, you may break it in two. But one poor fellow I saw was completely exhausted trying to break a hard tack, and after resorting to all the devices he could think of, finally accomplished it by dropping on it a 12-pound shell. The objection to that plan was, however, that the fellow could hardly find his hard tack afterward.

At midnight we crept out of camp unobserved—everything being quiet except now and then a shot on picket line.

JUNE 23D.—We halted this morning at six o'clock, and but a few minutes elapsed before two-thirds of the regiment were fast asleep. A few very hungry ones, only, made coffee and took breakfast.

We find ourselves again on the road to Jackson, but what our final destination is, no one knows except the *stars* in front. We surmise our course to be through Johnston's army, if we can find it.

The "blarsted" bugle blasted us out on the road again at seven.

Dog, or Shelter Tent.

I believe I, for one, would rather have spent my hour in eating t h a n sleeping. However, we trudged our eight miles at an easy pace and halted again. The birds were singing merrily, with no sounds of war to interfere. It is rumored that we are out hunting the paymaster instead of Johnston.

JUNE 24TH.—Awaiting orders to march is as tiresome as waiting at a station for a train. We were ready for marching orders again this morning, but failed to get them.

The weather is hot. Some of the rebel prisoners have said we could not stand this heat, but I guess the Yanks can stand it if they can, and if it should actually get too hot, we will just cool their country off. The nights are pleasant enough and we are thankful for the comfort of the sleep which they allow us. We have a chance out here to forage a little, and though but little, any change from army rations becomes agreeable.

It is amazing what progress soldiers make in foraging. They began committing such depredations as to cause an order on the subject to be issued, and on the eighth of May last the com-

FRICTION TUBE FOR FIRING CANNON.— The tube is inserted into the vent of the cannon and fired by means of a stout cord, which has a wooden handle at one end, and an iron hook at the other; the cannoneer puts the hook through the loop in the wire of the friction tube, and holding the cord by the handle, pulls steadily until the wire is withdrawn, when an explosion takes place, induced by the friction of the wire against the composition in the tube.

manding General required a general order, prohibiting foraging, to be read throughout the army five times a day. Not long after that, two soldiers of the 13th corps were arrested and brought before General A. J. Smith, at his headquarters in a fine grove of stately poplars, where the General was informed by the guard that the men had been caught in the act of stealing chickens. The gallant General appeared to be revolving the heinousness of the charge as he looked aloft among the poplars, and presently the guard inquired what should be done with the men, when the General, after another glance upward, turning to the guard, replied, "O, damn 'em, let 'em go. There ain't any tree here high enough to hang 'em on."

JUNE 25TH.—We have orders to stay in camp, ready to move at a moment's notice. Our marching orders are still delayed, so we have enjoyed a good rest. We are now out of hearing of the guns at Vicksburg, and it seems very still around us, indeed.

The term of the enlistment of some members of our regiment has now expired, and they seem to want to get home again to see their mamas; but go they can not until our "rabbit is caught." Shame on them for wanting to leave before the flag flies over Vicksburg. Many of them have had letters from friends at the North, urging them not to stay after their time is out. But they may as well make up their minds that Grant will hold them till Vicksburg is taken.

JUNE 26TH.—We have heard that Port Hudson is ours, and I hope this may be true, for it will tend to hasten the surrender of Vicksburg.

A little dirt has been thrown up ahead of us, as a shield, in case we have to fight the enemy. We hear all sorts of reports about the strength of Johnston's army, but the truth will only appear when we meet it. One captive said the report in Vicksburg was that Pemberton despaired of getting help from the out side, and was ready to sur-

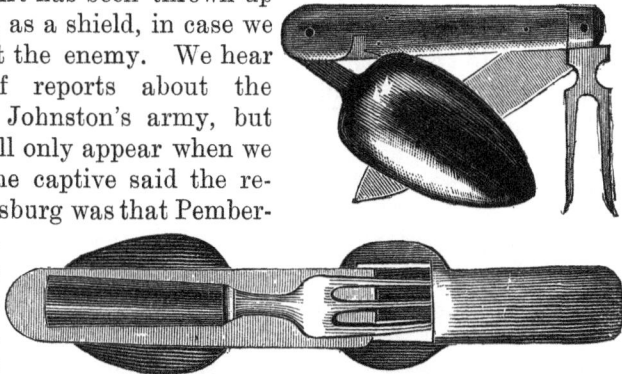

Combined knife, fork and spoon, used by the boys at the siege of Vicksburg.

render when the last meal rations have been eaten. He probably understands the resources of our commissary, as well as the magnanimous disposition of Grant to issue provisions to a starving foe.

—5

Well, why not? The first square meal received from Uncle Sam will be an occasion to them of thanksgiving. They will get the best that we can issue. And when the war is over, true soldiers of both armies will be among the first to break the bread of reunion and quaff the cup of restored peace and good will.

JUNE 27TH.—A number of our boys went a few miles, blackberrying, and picked quite a quantity to bring home, when we heard the sound of horses' hoofs, and suddenly concluding we had berries enough, we beat a hasty retreat for camp and got there safely.

The weather is not quite as hot here as it was in our close quarters at the front, but while we enjoy that change we would much prefer remaining at our post there, until the end of the siege.

Some of the boys have had to boil their pants—the only process which is sure death to an enemy lurking there which we find most troublesome. While our pants are boiling the owner leans over the kettle anxiously, for it is probably his only pair. Well, it is now summer time, and it will do to sun ourselves an hour or two. These little pests lurking in our pants become very annoying when they go foraging. These creatures are about the only war relics from which I have not gathered specimens to send home. I have, in fact, *gathered* enough of them, but with no view to a museum or cabinet. It is fun to see a fellow get into a pair of boiled pants. The boiling has shrunk them till they fail to reach the top of his brogans by some inches, and accordingly he bends over to try to pull them down to a junction, when the contrary things seem to recoil still further; and the only satisfaction left to him at last—and it is no mean one, either—is that they are at least clean, and he himself is once more their sole occupant. How long he will remain so, however, it is hard to say.

JUNE 28TH.—The boys of the 20th left at Vicksburg joined our regiment to-day. We were very anxious to hear how the siege was progressing, and, to our surprise, learned that it was going right on as usual, without our assistance. It was interesting to hear of the blowing up of Fort Hill by our division, but we did not ascertain the number killed, though the explosion

> Hoisted two or three,
> And blew a darky free
> From slavery to freedom.

This negro, blown up with other chattels in the fort, was dropped into our lines and taken to General Logan's headquarters, none the worse for his trip. When asked what he saw, he said, "As I was comin' down I met massa gwine up." Nothing, however, was gained by blowing up the fort, except planting the

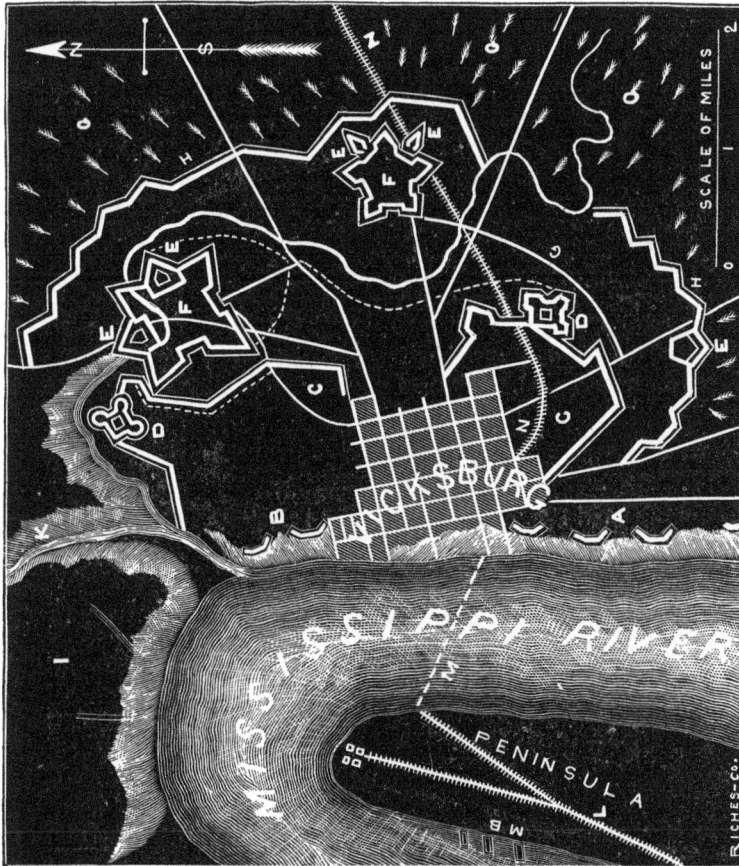

PLAN OF DEFENSES AT VICKSBURG.

EXPLANATIONS.

A. Lower Water Batteries.	H. Outer Lines of Defense.
B. Upper Water Batteries.	I. Walnut Bluffs.
C. Inner Lines of Defense.	K. Bayou.
D. Redoubt. (A Fortification breast high.)	L. Shreveport Railroad.
	M. Ferry.
E. Redan. (A Fortification in the shape of the letter A.)	M. B. Mortar Boats.
	N. Jackson Railroad.
F. Fort	O. Abattis. (Trees or branches of Trees to impede the approach of Assailants.)
G. Road.	
Dotted Lines. Rifle Pits.	

stars and stripes thereon, by our troops who made the charge
after the explosion ; but our colors were removed, for safety, after
dark. While our men lay all the afternoon on the side of the
fort, the rebels threw into their ranks hand-grenades which killed
and wounded quite a number. Our boys, however, would occasionally catch them and toss them back to the place from which
they came, just in time to explode among their owners.

Living out here in the woods is quite different from camping
before Vicksburg. Yet all is life and bustle wherever we are,
from reveille at daybreak, to tattoo at night. Each man must
answer to his name in ranks at roll-call in the morning, and must
be properly dressed. Some of the most ludicrous scenes of army
life are to be witnessed at this exercise. A few of the old fash-
ioned, steady fellows, as a general thing appear quite thoroughly
dressed ; but as you go down the ranks from the head where they
stand, you will begin to find, now and then, a man who has but
one boot or shoe on, with the other but half way on. Another
boy will be putting on his blouse—having grabbed it in the
dark—of course wrong side out. Another has tossed his blouse
over his shoulders, and is trying to hide close to his right-hand
man. Still another, trying to get his pants on between his bed
and the line, has caught a foot in the lining, and hops along like
a sore-footed chicken. I saw one fellow come out, at the foot of
the company, wrapped only in a blanket. The orderly, however,
sent him back to be better uniformed ; he could not play Indian
at morning roll-call. The last one of those who have over-
slept, makes his appearance holding on to his clothes with both
hands. Some answer to their names before taking position in
the ranks, and in fact, even some before they are fairly out of
bed. A company which has for its orderly a person who is a
little lenient, fares well ; but if he is inclined to strain his authority,
he is bound to have its ill-will. After roll-call, some of the
half-dressed return to bed for another snooze, while the rest complete their toilet. After that comes the splitting of rails, building
of fires, and a general rush for breakfast, which winds up the duties of the morning.

JUNE 29TH.—The 4th of July is fast approaching, and if we do
not get our prize by that time, we will have a little celebration
out here in the woods, for we have flags, drums and plenty of
spread-eagle speakers, and we can omit the cannon, of which

kind of music we have had a surfeit. Yes, we have all the material for a patriotic celebration, but I had hoped we should waive the old flag in Vicksburg that day.

I was sick last night, and up many times before day; and as I walked among the sleepers, I was astonished at the snoring; the variety of sounds made was as great as that of a brass band.

A rumor circulates that Pemberton has made an attack on our lines at Vicksburg, trying to cut his way out, but failed of his purpose. From a prisoner brought in, I have learned, by questioning, that the rebel authorities have made numerous drafts for young and old, to refill their ranks, and I think their army now must be as strong as it can ever be. By conscription and terrorism they have forced into the field every available man. With the North it is not so, for the old song, "We are Coming, Father Abraham, Three Hundred Thousand More," is being sung there yet, with good will, and volunteers are still pouring in to fill up what may be lacking in our ranks. We can thus throw renewed forces against failing ones.

JUNE 30TH.—Our dreams were broken this morning at daylight by the bug'e call, and in a very few minutes the whole command was up and ready to march—their beds around the owners' necks. Our wo len blankets are rolled up as tight as possible, having a rubber one outside, which, when the two ends are tied, are swung around our necks. If there has been a rain to wet the blankets, and no time to dry them, they make a heavy load on the march; so no time is lost in drying blankets whenever the opportunity is offered. If it is raining when we retire, and brush can be cut to lay the blankets on, we get a number one spring bed, and when the weather is pleasant a good bed can be made by laying down two rails the width of the blanket apart, and filling the space with grass, or straw from any adjacent stack, on which the blankets may be spread. There is a sort of tall grass growing in this country which makes a soft bed, and is quite worth the pulling. Everything possible is done by the soldier to secure a good night's sleep. I have seen straw stacks torn to pieces, sheds pulled down, and fences melt away in the twinkling of an eye, about camp time. A certain officer has ordered his men to take only the top rail, which order was obeyed to the letter, yet every rail disappeared—the bottom rail finally becoming the top one. I have

The charge and repulse at Fort Hill.

seen half a regiment bearing rails, boards and straw toward camp before even the end of the day's march was reached. They will have good beds and fires.

JULY 1ST. Here we enter upon the patriotic month of July, and where and how we are to spend it is yet beyond our conjecture, for we never know in this kind of service what a day may bring forth.

Preparations appear to have been made here for remaining in camp, and yet we may sleep to-night many miles away, or perhaps, without sleeping, march the whole night through. If only life is spared, it is enough; our duties are not shirked. If we camp only for a day, our quarters are to be all cleaned up, and everything put in the best order possible for comfort. On such excursions as this we have no mess cooking, but every fellow cooks for himself. The first man up in the morning, therefore, gets the frying-pan, from whom the next must engage it, and then may come number three, who is referred to number two.

So the utensil goes round a group or mess. The coffee is generally made in a camp kettle for the entire company. I have spent more time hunting up the owner of the last claim on the frying-pan than it afterward took to fry my bacon and crackers.

The pay-master is said to be not far from camp, which creates quite an excitement, since he may charge upon us any moment. There were orders for inspection every morning at eight o'clock for all companies. A little exercise of this kind hurts nobody. I took a stroll through the woods, looking at the graves of those who had fallen by the wayside while our army fought for the position it now holds around Vicksburg. These graves will soon be leveled, and their last trace lost. Friends may mourn for the fallen, but their tears will never water the graves of the heroes.

I write with the aid of a bayonet candle-stick. The latter end of this month will find me just twenty-one years of age.

JULY 2ND.—This is Camp Tiffin. Our regiment was favored to-day with a large mail, and nothing could have been more acceptable. Letters from home were looked into first, and next, of course, came sweethearts. One letter was read aloud, describing the capture of a butternut camp, in Holmes county, Ohio. The fort was built on a hill, and manned with several cannon, to resist the draft. A few soldiers from Camp Chase, however, went over and soon put an end to that attempt at resistance. I regret to hear of such a disgraceful affair occurring in my native State. From other letters and papers it appears this thing occurs in many other Northern States, and of course it must give encouragement to the rebels.

The rumor now runs that the paymaster will be at hand to-morrow, but he is about as reliable as Johnston, for we have been something like a week looking for both these gentlemen. I confess I would rather meet greenbacks than graybacks.

This afternoon, with several others, I went blackberrying again, and in searching for something to eat, we paid a visit to a house where, to our happy surprise, we found a birthday party, brightened by the presence of no less than eleven young ladies. We asked, of course, where "the boys" were, and they replied, as we expected, "out hunting Yanks." Well, we found it a treat to get a taste of sociality once more, after being so long famished. They were very nice rebel girls, though I think the color of the eyes of one of them was what I might call *true blue*. They asked us to lunch with them, which we did with pleasure. The eatables were good, and we had a splendid time—all the while, of course, keeping one eye on the girls and the other on the window. We told our experience at our last blackberrying excursion, when they assured as we had nothing to fear with them, for they were all "for the Union." No doubt they will be whenever their "boys" come home.

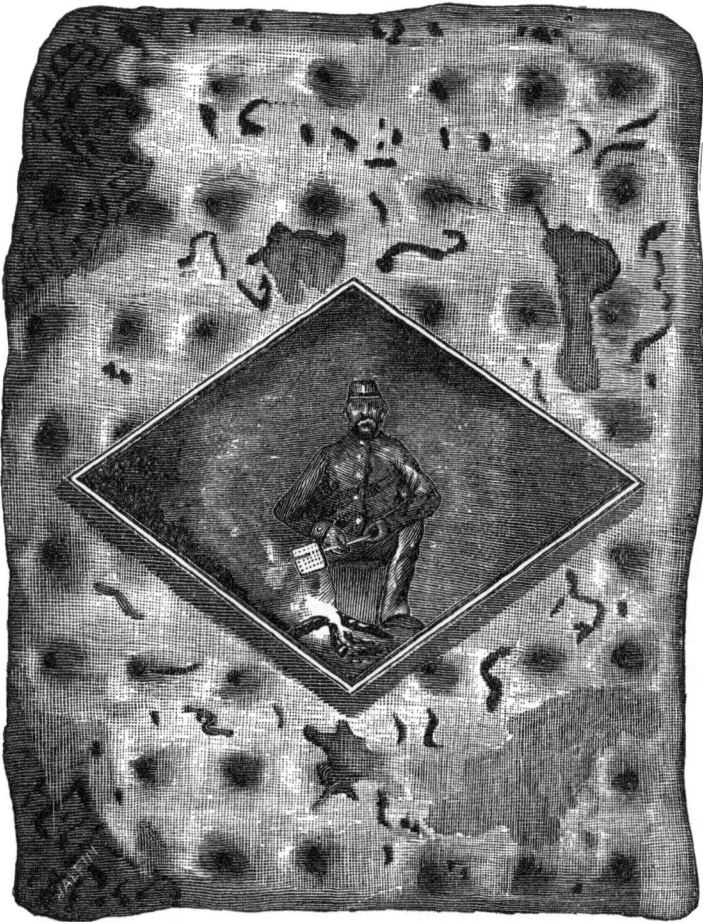

This is a fac-simile of a "hard-tack" issued to the author at Vicksburg. The scene upon it represents a soldier toasting his cracker, and the spots in the cracker were caused by the worms which inhabited it.

JULY 3D.—Uncle Sam's cashier has arrived at last, and we have been paid for two months' service. The married men are quite anxious to send their money home to their wives and little ones. It is risky sending money North from here, yet, to some, more dangerous to keep it. I saw two boys sitting on a log, to-day, playing poker at five cents a game. Five cent currency is paid in a sheet, and, as either lost the game, a five cent piece was torn off.

HE FOURTH OF JULY! The siege is at last ended. Behold the white flag now waving over the rebel ramparts. Vicksburg has at length surrendered. Speed the glad news to our loved ones at the North, who, during our long trial, have helped us with their prayers. Speed it to the entire forces of the Union, that they may all take courage and move again.

We are all full of rejoicing, as the event will no doubt prove a death-blow to the rebellion in the Southwest. Vicksburg has been the boast of the enemy, who thought it to be impregnable, and they confidently defied the Army of the West to take it. But by the untiring energy, skill and forecast of our gallant leader, U. S. Grant, aided by the willing and brave hearts about him, Vicksburg has been taken, and over it the stars and stripes now float proudly in all their majestic beauty. How glad I am that I have been one of those who have endured the trials requisite to plant our banner there. And while rejoicing over our success, let us not forget those who have died on these fields of honor. While we surviving raise Liberty's ensign over Vicksburg, let us remember the graves at Raymond and Champion Hills. And in after years, when we meet to refresh the memory of soldier days, let our dead here around Vicksburg never be forgotten. Let us think of them as standing guard over our dearly-won prize, until the final roll-call, when each shall be " present " or " accounted for."

"They struggled and fell, their life-blood staining
  The assaulting foeman's hand;
And clasping freedom's flag. sustaining,
  Cried, God save our native land.
Let angels spread their wings protecting;
  Let sweetest flowers ever bloom;
And let green bays, our faith reflecting,
  Mark each martyr's sacred tomb."

Now that the enemy have resigned possession of Vicksburg, I trust the wicked rebellion will not fail soon to near its end, when all our boys in blue will have leave, at will, *to present arms* to the girls they left behind them. A star heralding the coming peace already seems to twinkle in the sky. We rejoice not less over our triumph to-day because it was consummated upon the glorious Fourth. And while we rejoice for our country, we show no unworthy exultation over the fallen, to whom we extend the sympathy of victors.

Our division, under its commander, General Logan, marched into the city in triumph, and there took command and completed the long desired event—raising the star spangled banner over the court house cupola.

"The armies of the Union
  Round Vicksburg long had lain;
For forty-seven days and nights
  Besieging it in vain.

Then came the morning of the Fourth,
  Our Nation's jubilee—
Ah, could the news this hour go north—
  In Vicksburg soon we'll be.

The siege is done, the struggle past.
  On this eventful day
Glad triumph crowns us, as, at last,
  Our thanks to God we pay.

Above the vanquished walls I stand,
  My country, proud to see
The festive hosts, with flag and band,
  Parading gloriously.

O, glorious Fourth! O blissful day!
  How hearts of thousands swell
To see such toils such hopes repay,
  Such dangers end so well."

APPENDIXES.

Gen. John S. Bowen.   Col. Montgomery.   Gen. John C. Pemberton. | Gen. U. S. Grant.   Gen. James B. McPherson.   Gen. A. J. Smith.

SURRENDER OF VICKSBURG.

APPENDIX A.

CORRESPONDENCE BETWEEN GENERALS GRANT AND PEMBERTON, RELATING TO THE SURRENDER OF VICKSBURG.

Under a flag of truce, in the forenoon of July 3, General John S. Bowen and Col. Montgomery, A. A. G. on Gen. Pemberton's staff, brought the following dispatch:

HEADQUARTERS, VICKSBURG, July 3, 1863.

Major-General Grant, Commanding United States forces:

GENERAL:—I have the honor to propose to you an armistice for — hours, with a view to arranging terms for the capitulation of Vicksburg. To this end, if agreeable to you, I will appoint three commissioners, to meet a like number to be named by yourself, at such place and hour as you may find convenient. I make this proposition to save the further effusion of blood, which must otherwise be shed to a frightful extent, feeling myself fully able to maintain my position for a yet indefinite period. This communication will be handed you, under a flag of truce, by Major-General John S. Bowen.

Very respectfully, your obedient servant,

J. C. PEMBERTON.

General Grant's reply:

HEADQUARTERS DEPARTMENT OF TENNESSEE,
IN THE FIELD, NEAR VICKSBURG, July 3, 1863.

Lieut.-General J. C. Pemberton, Commanding Confederate forces:

GENERAL:—Your note of this date, just received, proposes an armistice of several hours for the purpose of arranging terms of capitulation, through commissioners to be appointed, etc. The effusion of blood you propose stopping by this course can be ended at any time you may choose, by an unconditional surrender of the city and garrison. Men who have shown so much endurance and courage as those now in Vicksburg will always challenge the respect of an adversary, and I can assure you will be treated with all the respect due them as prisoners of war. I do not favor the proposition of appointing commissioners to arrange terms of capitulation, because I have no other terms than those indicated above.

I am, General, very respectfully, your obedient servant,

U. S. GRANT, *Major-General.*

General Bowen requested that General Grant would meet General Pemberton on neutral ground, as more could be accomplished by a personal interview, to which General Grant replied he would meet General Pemberton in the afternoon, at three o'clock. At three o'clock General Pemberton made his appearance, accompanied by General John S. Bowen and Col. Montgomery, and at the same time Generals Grant, James B. McPherson and A. J. Smith passed through the Union line and met them beneath a large oak tree that stood between the two lines, and to the left of Fort Hill on the Jackson road. After a lengthy conversation, without settling upon any definite terms, the six officers returned to their respective quarters. General Grant sent the following dispatch by the hands of General John A. Logan and Lieutenant-Colonel Wilson:

Book made of the tree under which Grant and Pemberton met.

HEADQUARTERS DEPARTMENT OF TENNESSEE,
NEAR VICKSBURG, July 3, 1863.

Lieutenant-General J. C. Pemberton, Commanding Confederate forces, Vicksburg, Miss.:

GENERAL:—In conformity with the agreement of this afternoon, I will submit the following proposition for the surrender of the city of Vicksburg, public stores, etc. On your accepting the terms proposed, I will march in one division, as a guard, and take possession at eight o'clock to-morrow morning. As soon as paroles can be made out and signed by the officers and men, you will be allowed to march out of our lines, the officers taking with them their regimental clothing, and staff, field and cavalry officers one horse each. The rank and file will be allowed all their clothing, but no other property. If these conditions are accepted, any

amount of rations you may deem necessary can be taken from
the stores you now have, and also the necessary cooking utensils
for cooking them; thirty wagons also, counting two two-horse or
mule teams as one. You will be allowed to transport such articles
as can not be carried along. The same conditions will be allowed
to all sick and wounded officers and privates as fast as they become able to travel. The paroles for these latter must be signed,
however, while officers are present authorized to sign the roll of
prisoners.

I am, General, very respectfully, your obedient servant,

U. S. GRANT, *Major-General.*

HEADQUARTERS, VICKSBURG, July 3, 1863.

Major-General Grant, Commanding United States forces:

GENERAL :—I have the honor to acknowledge the receipt of your
communication of this date, proposing terms for the surrender of
this garrison and post. In the main, your terms are accepted;
but in justice both to the honor and spirit of my troops, manifested in the defense of Vicksburg, I have the honor to submit
the following amendments, which, if acceded to by you, will perfect the agreement between us : At ten o'clock to-morrow I propose to evacuate the works in and around Vicksburg, and to
surrender the city and garrison under my command, by marching
out with my colors and arms and stacking them in front of my
present limits, after which you will take possession; officers to
retain their side-arms and personal property, and the rights and
personal property of citizens to be respected.

I am, General, yours very respectfully,

J. C. PEMBERTON, *Lieutenant-General.*

General Grant replied as follows :

HEADQUARTERS DEPARTMENT OF TENNESSEE,
BEFORE VICKSBURG, July 4, 1863.

Lieutenant-General Pemberton, Commanding forces in Vicksburg:

GENERAL :—I have the honor to acknowledge your communication of the 3d of July. The amendments proposed by you can
not be acceded to in full. It will be necessary to furnish every
officer and man with a parole signed by himself, which, with the
completion of the rolls of prisoners, will necessarily take some
time. Again, I can make no stipulation with regard to the treatment of citizens and their private property. While I do not propose to cause any of them any undue annoyance or loss, I can

—3

not consent to leave myself under restraint by stipulations. The property which officers can be allowed to take with them will be as stated in the proposition of last evening —that is, that officers will be allowed their private baggage and side-arms, and mounted officers one horse each. If you mean by your proposition for each brigade to march to the front of the lines now occupied by it, and stack their arms at ten o'clock A. M., and then return to the inside and remain as prisoners until properly paroled, I will make no objection to it. Should no modifications be made of your acceptance of my terms by nine o'clock A. M., I shall regard them as having been rejected, and act accordingly. Should these terms be accepted, white flags will be displayed along your lines, to prevent such of my troops as may not have been notified from firing on your men.

I am, General, very respectfully, your obedient servant,

U. S. GRANT, *Major-General U. S. A.*

Pemberton's reply:

HEADQUARTERS, VICKSBURG, July 4, 1863.

Major-General U. S. Grant, Commanding United States forces, etc.:

GENERAL:—I have the honor to acknowledge the receipt of your communication of this date, and, in reply, to say that the terms proposed by you are accepted.

Very respectfully, your obedient servant,

J. C. PEMBERTON, *Lieutenant-General.*

Shortly after this dispatch was received, the white flags—the signals of surrender—waved along the entire line of the enemy. At one o'clock the line marched into Vicksburg, as follows:

Major-General U. S. Grant and staff.

Major-General James B. McPherson and staff.

Major-General John A. Logan and staff.

Brigadier-General M. D. Leggett, First Brigade, Third Division, led by the Forty-Fifth Illinois.

Brigadier-General Thomas E. G. Ransom, First Brigade, Seventh Division, temporarily assigned to Logan.

Brigadier-General John D. Stevenson, Second Brigade, Third Division.

The procession, arriving at the court house, placed the stars and stripes on its dome.

Vicksburg Court House, the target for a hundred guns.

INSIGNIA OF RANK IN THE U. S. ARMY.

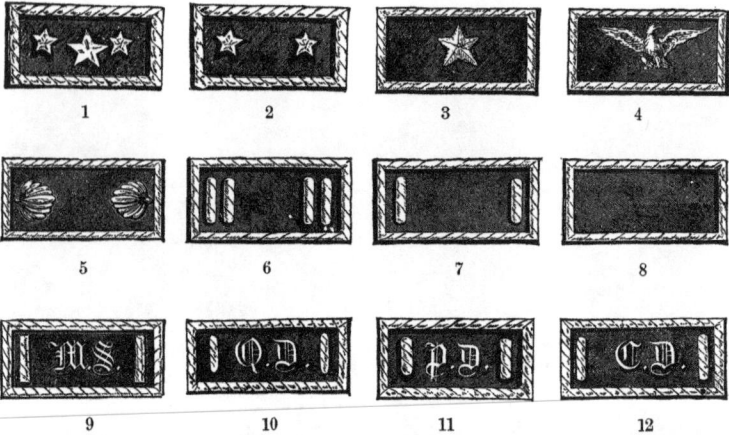

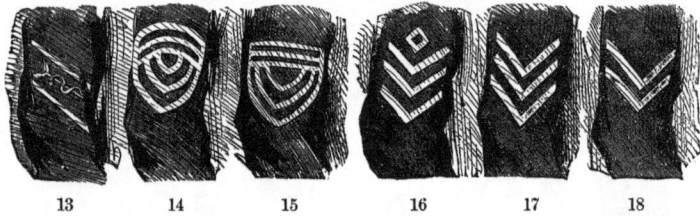

1,—Lieutenant-General.
2.—Major-General.
3.—Brigadier-General.
4.—Colonel.
5.—Lieutenant-Colonel, silver leaf, (Major, gold leaf.)
6.—Captain.
7.—First Lieutenant.
8.—Second Lieutenant.
9.—Surgeon, (Medical Staff.)
10.—Quartermaster, (Quartermaster Department.)
11.—Paymaster, (Paymaster Department.)
12.—Commissary, (Commissary Department.)
13.—Hospital Steward.
14.—Sergeant-Major.
15.—Quartermaster Sergeant.
16.—Orderly Sergeant.
17.—Second Sergeant.
18.—Corporal.
19.—Veteran—stripes for re-enlisting.

APPENDIX B.

ROSTER

OF THE

UNION FORCES OPERATING AGAINST VICKSBURG, MISSISSIPPI,

MAY 1ST, 1863—JULY 4TH. 1863.

ARMY OF THE TENNESSEE,

(Photo from life—1864.)

MAJ.-GEN'L ULYSSES S. GRANT.

ESCORT:

CAPTAIN E. D. OSBAND, Co. A, 4th Ill. Cav.

ENGINEER:

MAJOR WM. TWEEDDALE, 1st Battalion Engineer Regt. of the West.

13TH ARMY CORPS.

MAJ.-GEN'L JOHN A. McCLERNAND.

ESCORT:

CAPTAIN DAVID R. SPARKS, Co. L, 3d Ill. Cav.

MAJ.-GEN'L E. O. C. ORD.
(Superceding Maj.-Gen'l McClernand, June 19th.)

NINTH DIVISION.

BRIG.-GEN'L PETER J. OSTERHAUS.

First Brigade.

(1) BRIGADIER-GEN'L THEOPHILUS T. GARRARD.

(2) BRIG.-GEN'L ALBERT L. LEE. (May 18.)

(May 19th, was struck by a rifle-ball in the right cheek. The ball dislodged a few teeth and passed out through the back of his neck.)

(3) COL. JAMES KEIGWIN. (May 19.)

118th Ill. (mounted); 49th Ind.; 69th Ind.; 7th Ky.; 120th Ohio.

SECOND BRIGADE.

(1) COL. LIONEL A. SHELDON.   (2) COL. DANIEL W. LINDSLAY. (May 31.)
54th Ind.; 22d Ky.; 16th Ohio; 42d Ohio; 114th Ohio.

ARTILLERY.

7th Batt'y Mich. Lt. Art'y. and 1st Batt'y Wis. Lt. Art'y.

CAVALRY.

(May 31.)   Cos. A, E and K, 3d Ill. Cav.
(June 30.) Three companies 2d Ill. and seven companies 6th Mo. Cav.

TENTH DIVISION.

BRIG.-GEN'L ANDREW J. SMITH.
ESCORT:
Co. C, 4th Ind. Cav.

FIRST BRIGADE.

BRIG.-GEN'L STEPHEN G. BURBRIDGE.
16th Ind.; 60th Ind.; 67th Ind.; 83d Ohio; 96th Ohio; 23d Wis.

SECOND BRIGADE.

COL. WM. J. LANDRAM.

77th Ill.; 97th Ill.; 108th Ill.; 130th Ill.; 19th Ky.; 48th Ohio.

ARTILLERY.

Ill. Lt. Art'y; Chicago Mercantile Battery; Ohio Lt. Art'y; 17th Battery.

TWELFTH DIVISION.

BRIG.-GEN'L ALVIN P. HOVEY.

ESCORT:
Co. C, 1st Ind. Cav.

FIRST BRIGADE.

BRIG.-GEN'L GEORGE F. McGINNIS.

11th Ind.; 24th Ind.; 34th Ind.; 46th Ind.; 29th Wis.

SECOND BRIGADE.

COL. JAMES R. SLACK.

47th Ind.; 24th Iowa; 28th Iowa; 56th Ohio; 87th Ill. (June 30.)

ARTILLERY.

2d Ill. Lt. Art'y; Batt'y. A, 1st Mo. Lt. Art'y; Batt'y A, Ohio Lt. Art'y; 2d Batt'y, and 16th Batt'y.

FOURTEENTH DIVISION.

BRIG.-GEN'L EUGENE A. CARR.

ESCORT:

Co. G, 3d Ill. Cav.

FIRST BRIGADE.

(1) BRIG. GEN'L WM. P. BENTON.

(2) COL. HENRY D. WASHBURN. (May 31.)   COL. DAVID SHUNK. (June 27.)

33d Ill.; 99th Ill.; 8th Ind.; 18th Ind.; 1st U. S.

Second Brigade.

(1) Col. Wm. M. Stone.

(2) BRIG.-GEN'L MICHAEL K. LAWLER. (May 2.)
21st Iowa; 22d Iowa; 23d Iowa; 11th Wis.

ARTILLERY.

Ind. Lt. Art'y; 1st Batt'y; Iowa Lt. Art'y, 1st Batt'y; (May 31.) Batt'y A, 2d Ill Lt. Art'y.

CAVALRY.

Unattached—Cos. F, G, H, I, K, 2d Ill. Cav.; Patterson's Co. Ky. Inf. (Pioneers) Cos. B, E, F, G, H, I, K, 6th Mo. Cav.

15TH ARMY CORPS.

MAJ.-GEN'L WILLIAM T. SHERMAN.

FIRST DIVISION.

MAJ.-GEN'L FREDERICK STEELE.

FIRST BRIGADE.

(1) COL. FRANCIS H. MANTER.   (2) COL. BERNARD G. FARRAR.   (June 13.)
13th Ill.; 27th Mo.; 29th Mo.; 30th Mo.; 31st Mo.; 32d Mo.

SECOND BRIGADE.

COL. CHARLES R. WOODS.
25th Iowa; 31st Iowa; 3d Mo.; 12th Mo.; 17th Mo.; 76th Ohio.

THIRD BRIGADE.

BRIG.-GEN'L JOHN M. THAYER.
4th Iowa; 9th Iowa; 26th Iowa; 30th Iowa.

ARTILLERY.

Iowa Lt. Art'y; 1st Batt'y; 2d Mo. Lt. Art'y; Batt'y F; Ohio Lt. Art'y; 4th 'Batt'y.

CAVALRY.

Kane County, Ill., 3d Ill. Cav., Co. D.

SECOND DIVISION.

MAJ.-GEN'L FRANK P. BLAIR.

FIRST BRIGADE.

COL. GILES A. SMITH.

113th Ill.; 116th Ill.; 6th Mo.; 8th Mo.; 13th U. S. (1st Bat.)

SECOND BRIGADE.

(1) COL. THOMAS KILBY SMITH.

(2) BRIG.-GEN'L. J. A. J. LIGHTBURN. (May 24.)

55th Ill.; 127th Ill.; 83 Ind.; 54th Ohio; 57th Ohio.

THIRD BRIGADE.

BRIG.-GEN'L HUGH EWING.
30th Ohio; 37th Ohio; 47th Ohio; 4th West Va.

ARTILLERY.
Batt'y A, B, H, 1st Ill. Lt. Art'y; 8th Batt'y (Section) Ohio Lt. Art'y.

CAVALRY.
Thielemann's Ill. Battalion, Cos. A and B; Co. C, 10th Mo.

THIRD DIVISION.

BRIG.-GEN'L JAMES M. TUTTLE.

—7

First Brigade.

(1) BRIG.-GEN'L RALPH P. BUCKLAND.

(2) COL. WILLIAM L. McMILLEN. (June 22.)

114th Ill.; 93d Ind.; 72d Ohio; 95th Ohio.

Second Brigade.

BRIG.-GEN'L JOSEPH A. MOWER.

47th Ill.; 5th Minn.; 11th Mo.; 8th Wis.

Third Brigade.

(1) BRIG.-GEN'L CHARLES L. MATTHIES

(2) COL. JOSEPH J. WOODS. (June 1.)

8th Iowa; 12th Iowa; 35th Iowa.

ARTILLERY.

1st Ill. Lt. Art'y, Batt'y E; 2d Batt'y Iowa Lt. Art'y.

CAVALRY.

Unattached—4th Iowa Cav.

17TH ARMY CORPS.

MAJ.-GEN'L JAMES B. McPHERSON.

ESCORT:
CAPT. J. S. FOSTER, Co. C, 4th Ohio Cav.

THIRD DIVISION.

MAJ.-GEN'L JOHN A. LOGAN.

ESCORT:

CAPT. J. R. HOTALING, Co. A, 2d Ill. Cav.

FIRST BRIGADE.

(1) BRIG.-GEN. JOHN E. SMITH.

(2) BRIG.-GEN'L MORTIMER D. LEGGETT. (June 3.)

20th Ill.; 31st Ill.; 45th Ill.; 124th Ill.; 23d Ind.

SECOND BRIGADE.

(1) BRIG.-GEN'L ELIAS S. DENNIS.

2) BRIG.-GEN'L M. D. LEGGETT. (May 15.)

(3) COL. MANNING F. FORCE. (June 3.)

30th Ill.; 20th Ohio; 68th Ohio; 78th Ohio.

THIRD BRIGADE.

BRIG.-GEN'L JOHN D. STEVENSON.

8th Ill.; 17th Ill.; 81st Ill.; 7th Mo.; 32 Ohio.

ARTILLERY.

MAJ. CHARLES J. STOLBRAND.

Batt'y D, 1st Ill. Lt. Art'y; Batteries G and L, 2d Ill. Lt. Art'y; 8th Batt'y Mich. Lt. Art'y; 3d Batt'y Ohio Lt. Art'y.
Unattached—63d Ill. (May 31.)

SIXTH DIVISION.

BRIG.-GEN'L JOHN McARTHUR.
ESCORT:
Co. G, 11th Ill. Cav.

FIRST BRIGADE.
BRIG.-GEN'L HUGH T. REID.
1st Kansas (Mounted); 16th Wis.

SECOND BRIGADE.

BRIG. ' GEN'L THOMAS E. G. RANSOM.
11th Ill.; 72d Ill.; 95th Ill.; 14th Wis.; 17th Wis.; *18th Wis.

*18th Wis. assigned to 1st Brigade, 7th Division, May 13.

THIRD BRIGADE.

1) BRIG.-GEN'L MARCELLUS M. CROCKER.
(Assigned to the 7th Division May 2.)

(2) COL. WILLIAM HALL. (May 2.)
(3) COL. ALEXANDER CHAMBERS. (June 6.

11th Iowa; 13th Iowa; 15th Iowa; 16th Iowa.

ARTILLERY.
MAJ. THOMAS D. MAURICE.
Batt'y F; 2d Ill. Lt. Art'y; 1st Batt'y Minn. Lt. Art'y.
Batt'y C, 1st Mo. Lt. Art'y; 10th Batt'y Ohio Lt. Art'y.

SEVENTH DIVISION.

(1) COL. JOHN B. SANBORN.
2) BRIG.-GEN. MARCELLUS M. CROCKER. (May 2.)

(3) BRIG.-GEN'L ISAAC F. QUINBY. (May 17.)
(4) BRIG.-GEN'L. JOHN E. SMITH, (June 31.)

ESCORT:
Co. E, 2d Ill. Cav.; Co. F, 4th Mo. Cav.

FIRST BRIGADE.

(1) COL. JESSE I. ALEXANDER.   (2) COL. JOHN B. SANBORN. (May 2.)
48th Ind.; 59tn Ind.; 4th Minn.; (18th Wis., May 13.)

SECOND BRIGADE.

(1) COL. SAMUEL A. HOLMES.   (2) COL. GREEN B. RAUM. (June 10.)
59th Ill.; 17th Iowa; 10th Mo.; Co. E, 24th Mo.; 80th Ohio.

THIRD BRIGADE.

(1) COL. GEORGE B. BOOMER.   (2) COL. HOLDEN PUTNAM. (May 22.)

(3) BRIG.-GEN'L CHARLES L. MATTHIES. (June 2.)
93d Ill.; 5th Iowa; 10th Iowa; 26th Mo.

ARTILLERY.

(1) CAPT. FRANK C. SANDS.

(2) CAPT. HENRY DILLON. (June.)

Batt'y M. 1st Mo. Lt. Art'y; 11th Batt'y Ohio Lt. Art'y.
6th Batt'y Wis. Lt. Art'y; 12th Batt'y Wis. Lt. Art'y.

HERRON'S DIVISION.

MAJ.-GEN'L FRANCIS J. HERRON.

FIRST BRIGADE.

BRIG.-GEN'L WILLIAM VANDEVER.

37th Ill.; 26th Ind.; 20th Iowa; 34th Iowa: 38th Iowa.

ARTILLERY.

Batt'y˜E, 1st Mo. Lt. Art'y; Batt'y F, 1st Mo. Lt. Art'y.

SECOND BRIGADE.

BRIG.-GEN'L W. W. ORME.

94th Ill.; 19th Iowa; 20th Wis.

ARTILLERY.

Batt'y B, 1st Mo. Lt. Art'y.

COL. CYRUS BUSSEY.

Unattached—Cavalry, 5th Ill.; 3d Iowa; 2d Wis.

16TH ARMY CORPS.
(May 31, 1863.)

FOURTH DIVISION.

BRIG.-GEN'L JACOB G. LAUMAN.

FIRST BRIGADE.
COL. ISAAC G. PUGH.

41st Ill.; 53d Ill.; 3d Iowa; 33d Wis.

SECOND BRIGADE.
COL. CYRUS HALL.

14th Ill.; 15th Ill.; 47th Ill.; 76th Ill.; 53d Ind.

THIRD BRIGADE.
(1) COL. GEORGE E. BRYANT.   (2) COL. AMORY K. JOHNSON. (June 9.)

28th Ill.; 32d Ill.; 12th Wis. (June 9th, 53d Ind.)

ARTILLERY.
CAPT. GEORGE C. GUMBART.

2d Ill. Lt. Art'y; Batteries E and K, Ohio Lt. Art'y; 5th, 7th and 15th Batteries.

CAVALRY.
MAJ. JAMES G. WILSON, Cos. F and I, 15th Ill.

9TH ARMY CORPS.
(June 30, 1863.)

MAJ.-GEN'L JOHN G. PARKE.

FIRST DIVISION.

BRIG.-GEN'L THOMAS WELSH.

FIRST BRIGADE.

COL. HENRY BOWMAN.
36th Mass.; 17th Mich.; 27th Mich.; 45th Pa.

THIRD BRIGADE.
COL. DANIEL LEASURE.
2d Mich.; 8th Mich.; 20th Mich.; 79th N. Y.; 100th Pa.
ARTILLERY.
Batt'y D, Pa. Lt. Art'y.

SECOND DIVISION.

BRIG.-GEN'L ROBERT B. POTTER.

FIRST BRIGADE.

COL. SAMUEL G. GRIFFIN.

6th N. H.; 9th N. H.; 7th R. I.

SECOND BRIGADE.

BRIG.-GEN. EDWARD FERRERO.

35th Mass.; 11th N. H.; 51st N. Y.; 51st Pa.

THIRD BRIGADE.

COL. BENJAMIN C. CHRIST.

29th Mass.; 46th N. Y.; 50th Pa.

ARTILLERY.

Batt'y L, 2d N. Y. Lt. Art'y. Artillery Reserve—Batt'y E, 2d U. S. Art y.

16TH ARMY CORPS.

(June 30, 1853.

FIRST DIVISION.

BRIG.-GEN L W. SOOY SMITH.

FIRST BRIGADE.

COL. JOHN M. LOOMIS.

26th Ill.; 90th Ill.; 12th Ind.; 100th Ind.

SECOND BRIGADE.

COL. STEPHEN G. HICKS.

40th Ill.; 103d Ill.; 15th Mich.; 46th Ohio.

THIRD BRIGADE.

COL. JOSEPH R. COCKERILL.

97th Ind.; 99th Ind.; 53d Ohio; 70th Ohio.

FOURTH BRIGADE.

COL. WILLIAM W. SANFORD.

48th Ill; 49th Ill.; 119th Ill.; 6th Iowa.

ARTILLERY.

CAPT. WM. COGSWELL.

Batteries F, I and M, 1st Ill. Lt. Art'y; Cogswell's Batt'y, Ill. Lt. Art'y; 6th Batt'y Ind. Lt. Art'y.

CAVALRY.

Co. B, 7th Ill.

DISTRICT NORTHEAST LOUISIANA.

BRIG.-GEN'L ELIAS S. DENNIS,

63d Ill.; 108th Ill.; 120th Ill.; 131st Ill.

CAVALRY.

Cos. A, D, G and K, 10th Ill.

COLORED TROOPS.

Post of Millikins' Bend—COL. HIRAM SCOFIELD.

8th La.; 9th La.; 11th La.; 43th La.; 1st Miss.; 3d Miss.

Post of Goodrich's Landing—COL. WM. F. WOOD.

1st Ark.; 10th La.

PROVISIONAL DIVISION.

From McPherson's Corps, commanded by GEN. JOHN McARTHUR.
Composed of the First and Third Brigades of McArthur's Sixth Division, and the Second Brigade of Logan's Third Division.

FIRST BRIGADE.
McArthur's Sixth Division.
COL. HUGH T. REID.

SECOND BRIGADE.
Logan's Third Division.
COL. MANNING F. FORCE.

THIRD BRIGADE.
McArthur's Sixth Division.
COL. WILLIAM HALL.

PROVISIONAL DIVISION.

BRIG.-GEN'L. NATHAN KIMBALL.

ENGELMANN'S BRIGADE.
COL. ADOLPH ENGELMANN.
43d Ill.; 61st Ill.; 106th Ill.; 12th Mich.

RICHMOND'S BRIGADE.
COL. JONATHAN RICHMOND.
18th Ill.; 54th Ill.; 126th Ill.; 22d Ohio.

MONTGOMERY'S BRIGADE.
COL. MILTON MONTGOMERY.
40th Iowa; 3d Minn.; 25th Wis.; 27th Wis.

ARTILLERY.
11th Batt'y, Ohio Lt. Art'y.

APPENDIX C.

ROSTER
OF THE
CONFEDERATE ARMY OPERATING IN THE SIEGE OF VICKSBURG,
MAY 1ST, 1863—JULY 4TH, 1863.

ARMY OF THE MISSISSIPPI AND TENNESSEE.

GEN'L JOSEPH E. JOHNSTON, Commanding.

ARMY OF THE MISSISSIPPI.

LIEUTENANT-GEN'L JOHN C. PEMBERTON.

STEVENSON'S DIVISION.

MAJ.-GEN'L C. L. STEVENSON.

FIRST BRIGADE.

BRIG.-GEN'L SETH M. BARTON.

40th Ga., COL. ABDA JOHNSON; 41st Ga., COL. W. E. CURTIS.
42d Ga., COL. R. J. HENDERSON; 52 Ga., COL. C. D. PHILLIPS.

SECOND BRIGADE.

BRIG.-GEN'L E. D. TRACY.

(Killed at the battle of Port Gibson, May 1.)

20th Ala., COL. ISHAM W. GARROTT; 23d Ala., COL. F. K. BECK.
30th Ala., COL. C. M. SHELLEY; 46th Ala., COL. M. L. WOODS.

THIRD BRIGADE.

BRIG.-GEN'L THOMAS H. TAYLOR.

57th Ga., COL. WM. BARKULOO; 39th Ga., COL. J. T. McCONNELL.
36th Ga., COL. JESSE A. GLENN; 56th Ga., COL. E. P. WATKINS.
34th Ga., COL. J. A. W. JOHNSON; 43d Tenn., COL. JAMES W. GILLESPIE.

FOURTH BRIGADE.

COL. A. W. REYNOLDS.

31st Tenn., COL. W. M. BRADFORD. (Known as 39th after June 6, 1863.)
59th Tenn., LIEUT.-COL. W. L. EAKIN.
3d Tenn., COL. N. J. LILLARD.

UNATTACHED COMPANIES.

Waddell's Lt. Batt'y, CAPT. JAMES F. WADDELL.
Cherokee Lt. Batt'y, CAPT. MAX VAN D. CORPUT.
Botetourt Lt. Batt'y, CAPT. J. W. JOHNSON.
3d Md. Batt'y, CAPT. F. O. CLAIBORNE.
Vandyke's Cav'y, CAPT. R. S. VANDYKE.

SMITH'S DIVISION.

MAJ.-GEN'L MARTIN L. SMITH.

First Brigade.

BRIG.-GEN'L W. E. BALDWIN.

31st La., Col. C. H. Morrison; 17th La., Col. R. Richardson.
4th Miss., Col. P. S. Layton; 46th Miss., Col. C. W. Sears.
Co. E, Miss. Lt. Art'y, Capt. Newitt J. Drew.
Partisan Rangers, Capt. S. J. Smith.

Second Brigade.

BRIG.-GEN'L JOHN C. VAUGHN.

79th [60th] Tenn., Col. J. H. Crawford.
80th [62d] Tenn., Col. John A. Rowan.
81st [61st] Tenn., Col. F. E. Pitts.
Ward's Art'y Batt'y, Maj. M. S. Ward; Co. A, Capt. C. B. Vance; Co. B, Capt. J. H. Yates.
Withers' Lt. Art'y, Co. I, Capt. Robert Bowman.

Third Brigade.

BRIG.-GEN'L F. A. SHOUP.

26th La., Col. W. Hall; 27th La., Col. L. D. Marks.
28th La., Col. Allen Thomas.
1st La. H'vy Art'y, Col. C. A. Fuller.
8th La. H'vy Art'y, Maj. F. N. Ogden.
1st Tenn. H'vy Art'y, Col. A. Jackson, Jr.
22d La. H'vy Art'y, Col. Isaac W. Patterson.
Capt. J. P. Lynch's Co. and Capt. J. Johnson's Co.

FORNEY'S DIVISION.

MAJ.-GEN'L JOHN H. FORNEY.

BRIG.-GEN'L LOUIS HEBERT'S BRIGADE.

3d La., Col. F. C. Armstrong.
36th Miss., Col. W. W. Witherspoon; 37th Miss., Col. O. S. Holland.
38th Miss., Col. Preston Brent; 43d Miss., Col. R. Harrison.
Hogg's [Tenn.] Batt'y, Capt. Wm. A. Hogg.

TILGHMAN'S BRIGADE.

BRIG.-GEN'L LOYD TILGHMAN.

(Killed at the battle of Champion Hills, May 16th, 1863.·

20th Miss., COL. D. R. RUSSELL.
26th Miss., COL. A. E. REYNOLDS.
54th Ala. (formerly 50th Ala.), COL. ALPHEUS BAKER.
8th Ky., COL. H. B. LYON.
23d Miss., COL. J. M. WELLS.
McLendon's Batt'y, CAPT. JACOB CULBERTSON (temporarily).

BRIG.-GEN'L. JOHN S. BOWEN'S DIVISION.

First Brigade.

COL. FRANCIS M. COCKRELL.

1st Mo., Lieut.-Col. A. C. Riley; 3d Mo., Lieut.-Col. F. L. Hubbell.
2d Mo., Col. F. M. Cockrell; 4th Mo., Col. A. McFarlane.
6th Mo., Col. Eugene Erwin; 5th Mo., Col. James McCown.
Wade's Batt'y, 1st Lieut. Richard C. Walsh.
Landis' Batt'y, Capt. John C. Landis.
Guibor's Batt'y, Capt. Henry Guibor.
Co. A, 1st La. H'vy Art'y, Capt. Jno. B. Grayson.

Second Brigade.

BRIG.-GEN'L MARTIN E. GREEN.
(Killed at Vicksburg, June 27th, 1863.)

1st Mo. Cav. (dismounted), COL. E. YATES.
3d Mo. Cav. (dismounted), LIEUT.-COL. D. F. SAMUEL.
15th Ark., LIEUT.-COL. W. W. REYNOLDS.
19th Ark., COL. D. W. JONES; 21st Ark., COL. J. E. CRAVENS.
1st Ark. Cav. (s. s.), CAPT. W. S. CATTERSON.
12th Ark. Inft. (s. s.), CAPT. GRIFF PAYNE.
Lowe's [Mo.] Batt'y, CAPT. SCHUYLER LOWE.
Dawson's [Mo.] Batt'y, CAPT. WM. E. DAWSON.
Western Rangers (Cav.), CAPT. P. M. SAVERY.

THIRD MILITARY DISTRICT.

(Headquarters, Port Hudson, La.)

MAJ.-GEN'L FRANK GARDNER, COMMANDING.

Maxey's Brigade.

BRIG.-GEN'L S. B. MAXEY.

42d Tenn., LIEUT.-COL. ISAAC N. HULME.
53d Tenn., CAPT. H. H. AYMETT.
55th Tenn.,
46th Tenn., } COL. A. J. BROWN.
48th Tenn., COL. W. M. VOORHIES; 49th Tenn., COL. J. E. BAILEY.
4th La., COL. S. E. HUNTER; 30th La., MAJ. C. J. BELL.
Batt'n [Texas] Sharpshooters, MAJ. JAMES BURNETT.
Fenner's [La.] Lt. Batt'y, CAPT. C. E. FENNER.
Roberts' [Miss.] Lt. Batt'y, CAPT. CALVIT ROBERTS.

Beall's Brigade.

BRIG.-GEN'L W. N. R. BEALL.

11th Ark. (c), COL. JOHN L. LOGAN.
17th Ark. (c), COL. JOHN GRIFFITH.

14th Ark. (d), Col. F. P. Powers; 18th Ark.; (d), Col. R. H. Crockett.
23d Ark. (d), Col. O. P. Lyles; 15th Ark. (e), Col. B. M. Johnson.
16th Ark. (e), Col. David Provence.
1st [8th] Batt. (e), Lieut.-Col. Bart Jones.
12th Ark., Col. T. J. Reid.
    (c) Consolidated, and commanded by Col. Logan.
    (d) Consolidated, and commanded by Col. O. P. Lyles.
    (e) Consolidated, and commanded by Col. B. W. Johnson.
1st Miss., Col. J. M. Simonton; 39th Miss., Col. W. B. Shelby.
Co. B, 1st Miss. Lt. Art'y (Withers' Art'y), Capt. A. J. Herod.
Co. F, 1st Miss. Lt. Art'y (Withers' Art'y), Capt. J. L. Bradford.
Co. K, 1st Miss. Lt. Art'y (Withers' Art'y), Capt. Geo. F. Abbay.

Gregg's Brigade.

BRIG.-GEN'L JOHN GREGG.

7th Texas, Maj. K. M. Vanzandt; 3d Tenn. (g), Col. C. H. Walker.
10th Tenn. (g), Col. R. W. McGavock; 30th Tenn. (g), Lieut.-Col. J. J. Turner.
41st Tenn. (h), Col. R. Farquharson; 50th Tenn. (h), Col. C. A. Sugg.
51st Tenn. (h), Co. G., Capt. John G. Hall; 1st Tenn. Batt'y (h), Maj. S. H. Colms.
9th La. Batt'y, Capt. H. M. Bledsoe.
Brook Haven Batt'y, Capt. James A. Hoskins.
    (g) Consolidated, and commanded by Col. MacGarock.
    (h) Consolidated, and commanded by Lieut.-Col. Beaumont.

Rust's Brigade.

BRIG.-GEN'L ALBERT RUST.

12th La., Col. T. M. Scott; 9th Ark., Col. Isaac L. Dunlop.
15th Miss., Lieut.-Col. J. R. Binford; 6th Miss., Col. R. Lowry.
35th Ala., Lieut.-Col. Ed. Goodwin.
1st Confederate Batt'y, Maj. G. H. Forney.
Hudson's Batt'y, Lieut.-Col. J. R. Iovancy.
Co. A, Point Coupie Art'y, Lieut. Charles L. Ilsley.
Co. C, Point Coupie Art'y, Capt. Alexander Churst.

Buford's Brigade.

BRIG.-GEN'L A. B. BUFORD.

3d Ky., Col. A. P. Thompson; 7th Ky., Col. Ed. Crossland.
10th Ark., Col. A. R. Witt; 49th Ala., Col. J. Edwards.
27th Ala., Col. James Jackson.
4th [16th] Ala. Batt'n (i), Lieut.-Col. John Snodgrass.
6th Ala. Batt'n, Major J. H. Norwood.
Watson Batt'y, Lieut. E. A. Toledano.

HEAVY ARTILLERY.

1st Ala. Reg't, Col. J. G. W. Steedman.
12th La. Batt'y, 1st Tenn. Batt'y, Lieut.-Col. P. F. DeGournay.
9th Tenn. Batt'y, Lieut.-Col. G. Gantt.
Hughes' Batt'y, Lieut.-Col. C. C. Wilburn.
Stockdale's Co. (j); Cage's Co. (j).
Daigri's Co. (j); Terrell's Co. (j); Bryant's (j).
(j) Consolidated, and commanded by Lieut.-Col. Snodgrass.
9th La. Batt'y, Col. J. H. Wingfield.
Garland's [Miss.] Batt'y, Maj. W. H. Garland.
Rhodes' [Miss.] Co. (K), Capt. T. C. Rhodes.
Herrin's Co. (C); Lester's Co. (l).
(k) Maj. Garland, commanding.
(l) Lieut.-Col. Miller, commanding.

FOURTH MILITARY DIVISION.

(Headquarters: Jackson, Miss.)

BRIG.-GEN'L JOHN ADAMS, Commanding.

Third Brigade.

(Mississippi State Troops.)

BRIG.-GEN'L J. L. GEORGE.

14th Miss. Reg't, Col. G. W. Abert.
1st Batt'n Choctaw Indians, Maj. J. W. Pierce.
1st Batt'n Miss. State Troops, Maj. W. B. Harper.
Bolen's Cav. Co., Capt. J. N. Bolen.
Terry's Cav. Co., Capt. B. D. Terry.
Co. C, 15th Miss., Capt. P. H. Norton.

FIRST MILITARY DISTRICT.

(Headquarters at Columbus, Miss.)

BRIG.-GEN'L DANIEL RUGGLES, Commanding.

Rice's Tenn. Heavy Art'y, Capt. T. W. Rice.
Thrall's Ark. Lt. Art'y, Capt. J. C. Thrall.
Owens' Ark. Lt. Art'y, Capt. J. A. Owens.
13th Batt'n Ala. Partisan Rangers, Maj. W. A. Hewlett.
3d Batt'n Miss. State Troops, Lieut.-Col. T. A. Burgin.
5th Reg't Miss. State Troops, Col. H. C. Robinson.
Gillelyn's Miss. Cav. (State Troops), Capt. D. C. Gillelyn.
Martin's Cav. Co. Capt. W. C. Martin.
Johnson's Cav. Co., Capt. J. E. Johnson.
2d Tenn. Cav., Lieut.-Col. C. R. Bartearn.
Warren's (Miss.) P. R., Capt. Isham I. Warren.

MOORE'S BRIGADE.

BRIG.-GEN'L JOHN C. MOORE.

35th Miss., COL. W. S. BARRY; 42d Ala., COL. JOHN W. PORTIS.
2d Texas, COL. ASHBEL SMITH; 40th Miss., COL. W. B. COLBERT.
37th Ala., COL. JAMES F. DOWDELL; Bledsoe's Batt'y, CAPT. H. M. BLEDSOE.
Pioneer Co., COL. LAUN; Tobin's Batt'y, CAPT. T. F. TOBIN.
Section Point Coupie Art'y, CAPT. DAVIDSON.
Sengstake's Batt'y, CAPT. HENRY H. SENGSTAKE.
McNally's Batt'y, CAPT. MCNALLY.
Section Point Coupie Art'y, LIEUT. JEFF J. THOMPSON.
Waul's Tex. Legion, LIEUT.-COL. LEONIDAS WILLIS.
Adams' Cavalry, COL. WIRT ADAMS.
1st [7th] Tenn. Cav., COL. J. G. STOCKS.

BRIG.-GEN'L STEPHEN D. LEE.
Commanding Brigade, Siege of Vicksburg.

BRIG.-GEN'L W. S. FEATHERSTONE.
Commanding Brigade in Gen. Loring's Division.

APPENDIX D.

RUNNING THE BATTERIES.

ADMIRAL DAVID D. PORTER,
(Commanding the Mississippi Squadron.)

U. S. GRANT'S OFFICIAL REPORT.

"The successful performance of this difficult and dangerous task was one of the most brilliant operations of the war. On the 16th of April, Admiral Porter was ready to make the first attempt. In this three transports were used—the Forest Queen, Henry Clay and Silver Wave—which were loaded with supplies, and their machinery protected by bales of cotton and hay. Together with these, eight gunboats, all iron-clad except one, and all further protected with cotton and hay bales, formed the little fleet to make the first trial, which took place at night. The gunboats were to proceed in single file, engaging the enemy's batteries if discovered and fired upon, while the transports were

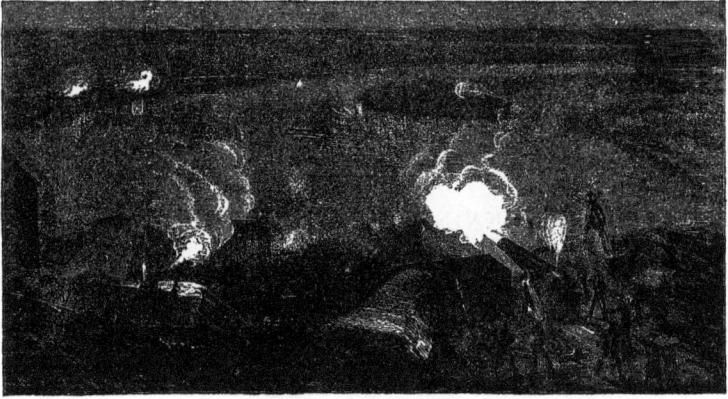

Passing the Batteries at Vicksburg.

to try and slip down the stream, under the cover of the smoke, between the gunboats and the opposite bank. It was between ten and eleven o'clock at night when they came around the bend of the river, and for a short time they supposed they were going to slip by unnoticed ; but all of a sudden two sharp and brilliant lines of fire gave the signal, and in an instant the whole length of the bluff was ablaze with the lurid flames of cannon. The gunboats returned the fire bravely, and in an hour and a quarter the batteries were passed. The damage done was as follows : The Forest Queen had received a shot through her steam-drum, but was towed safely past, and soon repaired. The Henry Clay was the worst sufferer ; her protection of cotton bales was set on fire, and she was abandoned, a blazing wreck, to float at the mercy of the stream. The fire of the gunboats so intimidated the batteries at Warrenton, that they scarcely responded.

"Inspired by this success, six more transports were got ready, towing twelve barges loaded with forage and rations ; and these were run by on the night of the 22d of April, from Milliken's Bend, and five of them succeeded in arriving below Vicksburg, but in a somewhat damaged condition, as follows : *Tigress, Anglo-Saxon, Chesseman, Empire City, Horizona,* and *Moderator.* The *Tigress* received a shot in her hull below the water line, and sunk on the Louisiana shore soon after passing the last of the batteries. With the exception of the *Forest Queen,* Captain D. Conway, and the *Silver Wave,* Captain McMillen, the crews were composed of volunteers. [Upon the call for volunteers to run these transports, officers and men presented themselves in numbers sufficient to run a hundred transports, caring but little for the dangerous enterprise.] Six out of the twelve barges loaded with forage and rations sent in tow of the last six boats, got through in a condition to be used.

"It is a striking feature, so far as my observation goes, of the present volunteer army of the United States, that there is nothing which men are called upon to do, mechanical or professional, that accomplished adepts cannot be found for the duty required, in almost every regiment."

Digging a canal across the peninsula on the Louisiana side of the river, in order to carry the army and supplies below Vicksburg, but which proved a failure. Located by Brigadier-General Williams.

The Gun boats running past the Vicksburg Batteries.

Pouring a Broadside at Grand Gulf.

—9

APPENDIX E.

LOSSES SUSTAINED IN THE OPERATIONS AGAINST VICKSBURG, FROM
MAY 1, 1863, TO JULY 4, 1863.

UNION FORCES.

	KILLED.	WOUNDED.	MISSING.	TOTAL.
Port Gibson, May 1...	130	718	5	853
Raymond, May 12.....	73	365	32	470
Jackson, May 14......	40	240	6	286
Champion Hill, May 16.	426	1,842	189	2,460
Big Black R'y. Bridge, May 17.............	29	242	2	273
Siege, May 19 to July 4.	245	3,688	303	4,536
Total............	943	7,095	537	8,878

CONFEDERATE FORCES.

One Lieutenant-General, John C. Pemberton, late Commander of the Army in Vicksburg.

Nineteen Major and Brigadier-Generals.

Forty-six thousand four hundred and twenty killed, wounded, stragglers and prisoners.

Ninety siege guns.

One hundred and twenty field pieces.

Thirty-five thousand muskets and rifles.

APPENDIX F.

CONFEDERATE ORDERS.

HEADQUARTERS SMITH'S DIVISION,
VICKSBURG, MISS., May 24th, 1863.

GENERAL:—Maj.-Gen'l Smith directs that you order the officers commanding the pickets to collect all the ammunition scattered in front of the trenches, and in the cartridge boxes of the enemy's dead, paying particular attention to the percussion caps; and that if the picket force is not sufficient you detail additional men for this purpose.

I am, General, very respectfully,
Your obedient servant,
JOHN G. DEVEREUX,
A. A. G.

BRIG.-GEN'L VAUGHN,
Commanding 2d Brigade.

HEADQUARTERS SMITH'S DIVISION,
VICKSBURG, MISS., May 25th, 1863.

GENERAL:—Should the enemy accept Gen'l Pemberton's proposition to suspend hostilities until they can bury their dead, no officer will be allowed to approach our lines; and at or near points they have assaulted, the bodies will be carried away and delivered by our men.

By command of
Major-General M. L. Smith,
JOHN G. DEVEREUX,
A. A. G.

BRIG.-GEN'L VAUGHN,
Commanding 2d Brigade.

DIVISION HEADQUARTERS,
VICKSBURG, MISS., May 25th, 1863.

GENERAL:—A flag of truce regarding the burial of the enemy's dead has been sent by General Pemberton, who directs that should they cease firing along their lines, there will be no firing along ours.

Respectfully, etc.,
M. L. SMITH,
Major-General.

GEN'L VAUGHN,
Commanding 2d Brigade.

The officers in command of troops in this Brigade will conform strictly with the accompanying order.

By order of Brig.-Gen'l Vaughn,
JOHN TOLAND,
A. A. A. G.

HEADQUARTERS SMITH'S DIVISION,
VICKSBURG, MISS., 29 May, 1863.

GENERAL:—Major-Gen'l Smith instructs me to inform you of the probability of a general assault to-night on all points, and to direct you to hold yourself in readiness to meet the same by cautioning the troops and requiring the pickets to be specially watchful.

Very respectfully,
Your obedient servant,
JOHN G. DEVEREUX,
A. A. G.

BRIG.-GEN'L J. C. VAUGHN,
Commanding 2d Brigade.

APPENDIX G.

REMINISCENCES OF THE THIRD LOUISIANA (CONFEDERATE) INFANTRY IN THE TRENCHES IN FRONT OF LOGAN'S DIVISION.

BY W. H. TUNNARD.

The regiment was placed near the centre of the line, on the left of the Jackson road, as it emerges from a deep cut through a hill. On the right of the road were the Twenty-first and Twenty-second Louisiana regiments, consolidated, and on their left the Mississippi regiments, comprising the remainder of Hebert's Brigade. General Hebert informed the men that they held the key to the city, on the most exposed portion of the line. The regiment responded that they would sustain their blood-earned reputation, justify the confidence reposed in their bravery, and perish to a man ere they would relinquish their position to a million foes. The enemy, in front of the Third regiment, were slowly but surely contracting their lines, and the fire of their sharpshooters was particularly accurate and deadly. Their batteries concentrated their fire on every one of our guns that opened on their lines, and speedily dismounted them. It was a foolhardy piece of business to expose the least portion of the person above the breastworks, as a hundred rifles immediately directed their missiles upon the man thus showing himself. In conversation with the enemy (then a common occurrence, from the proximity of the lines), a member of Company E, by the name of Masterton, a Missourian of huge dimension, and familiarly known in the regiment as "Shanghai," found some acquaintances, and was invited into the enemy's lines, with the assurance that he would be allowed to return. The invitation was immediately accepted, and he trusted himself to the honor of the foe. He was cordially welcomed, and all the delicacies and substantials which the Federals possessed in such profusion were furnished him. After a feast, accompanied with a sociable chat and several drinks, he was permitted to return, very favorably impressed with the generosity of the Yankees. The evening chats, after the day's deadly sharpshooting, revealed the fact that there were members of both armies who were personally acquainted, and, in one instance, two members of the Third regiment found a brother in the regiment opposed to them.

The report of a single gun within the breastworks was the signal for a concentrated fire of the enemy's batteries, which poured a perfect storm of shot and shell upon the fated point, resulting, usually, in the destruction of the battery, and killing and wounding numbers of the artillerymen. No less than five cannoniers were shot in an attempt to apply a lighted fuse to the vent of a loaded gun. Nearly all the artillery along the lines was dismounted by the furious bombardment of the 22d. General Grant sent in a flag of truce, asking permission to bury his dead, which were lying unburied in thick profusion outside of the intrenchments, where the enemy had assaulted the lines. General Pemberton refused to grant the request, replying that the battle was not yet decided. The enemy commenced undermining our parapet, with the intention of blowing it up. As the sound of their voices could be distinctly heard, our brave boys began to annoy them by hurl'ng upon them every species of deadly missile which human ingenuity could invent. 12-pounder shells were dropped over the breastworks among them, and kegs filled with powder, shells, nails and scraps of iron. A more deadly, vindictive and determined species of warfare was never waged. The chief aim of both combatants seemed to be concentrated in the invention of apparatus for taking human life. In the afternoon of May 25th, a flag of truce was sent into the lines, requesting a cessation of hostilities for the purpose of burying the dead, and the request was granted for three hours.

Now commenced a strange spectacle in this thrilling drama of war. Flags were displayed along both lines, and the troops thronged the breastworks, gaily chatting with each other; discussing the issues of the war; disputing over differences of opinion, losses in the fights, etc. Numbers of the Confederates accepted invitations to visit the enemy's lines, where they were hospitably entertained and warmly welcomed. They were abundantly supplied with provisions and supplies of various kinds.

Of course, there were numerous laughable and interesting incidents resulting from these visits. The foe were exultant, confident of success, and in high spirits; the Confederates defiant, undaunted in soul, and equally well assured of a successful defense. The members of the Third Regiment found numerous acquaintances and relatives among the Ohio, Illinois and Missouri regiments, and there were mutual regrets that the issues of the war had made them antagonistic in a deadly struggle. Captain F. Gallagher, the worthy commissary of the regiment, had been enjoying the hospitalities of a Yankee officer, imbibing his fine liquors and partaking of his choice viands, and as they separated, the Federal remarked: "Good day, Captain; I trust we shall meet soon again in the Union of old." Captain G., with a peculiar expression on his pleasant face, and an extra side poise of his head, quickly replied: "I can not return your sentiment. The only union which you and I will enjoy, I hope, will be in kingdom come; good bye, sir." At the expiration of the appointed time, the men were all back in their places. The stillness which had superseded the uproar of battle seemed strange and unnatural. The hours of peace had scarcely expired ere those who had so lately intermingled in friendly intercourse were once again engaged in the deadly struggle. Heavy mortars, artillery of every calibre, and small arms, once more with thunder-tones awakened the slumbering echoes of the hills surrounding the heroic city of Vicksburg. The constant daily fighting, night work, and disturbed rest, began to exhibit their effects on the men. They were physically worn out and much reduced in flesh. Rations began to be shortened, and for the first time (May 30) a mixture of ground peas and meal was issued. This food was very unhealthy, as it was almost impossible to thoroughly bake the mixture so that pea-flour and meal would be fit for consumption. Yet these deficiencies were heroically endured, and the men succeeded, by an ingenious application of the culinary art, in rendering this unwholesome food palatable, calling the dish "cush-cush." June 4th, the rations furnished each man was: Peas, one-third of a pound; meal, two-thirds to five-sixths of a pound; beef, one-half of a pound, including in the weight bones and shanks; sugar, lard, soap and salt in like proportions.

On this day all surplus provisions in the city were seized, and rations issued to citizens and soldiers alike. To the perils of the siege began now to be added the prospects of famine. The gaunt skeleton of starvation commenced to appear among the ranks of the brave defenders.

It seems wonderful that human endurance could withstand the accumulated horrors of the situation. Living on this slender allowance, fighting all day in the hot summer's sun, and at night, with pick-axe and spade, repairing the destroyed portions of the line, it passed all comprehension how the men endured the trying ordeal.

The city was rife with rumors (June 6), among which was the report of Johnston approaching with succor. The story almost gained credence by the report of cannon being heard toward Big Black. The welcome sounds were received with shouts along the whole line. Long, anxiously, eagerly, had the men been listening for the welcome signal, and now felt as if relief had assuredly come. Ah! on what a slender thread does an expectant soul hang its feeble hopes!

The Federals procured a car-frame, which they placed on wheels, loading it with cotton bales. They pushed this along the Jackson road, in front of the breastworks held by the Third regiment. Protected by this novel, movable shelter, they constructed their works with impunity, and with almost the certainty of eventually reaching our intrenchments. Rifles had no effect on the cotton bales, and there was not a single piece of artillery to batter them down. They were not a hundred yards from the regiment, and the men could only quietly watch their operations, and anxiously await the approaching hand-to-hand struggle. There was no shrinking or quailing; danger had long since ceased to cause any fear, and fighting was a recreation and pastime with the majority of the men. Exploding shells and whistling bullets attracted but little notice. Even death had become so familiar, that the fall of a comrade was looked upon with almost stoical indifference—eliciting, perhaps, a monosyllabic expression of pity, and most generally the remark, "I wonder who will be the next one." Men are not naturally indifferent to danger, nor do their hearts usually exhibit such stoical indifference to human agony and suffering; yet the occurrence of daily scenes of horror and bloodshed through which they passed, the shadow of the angel of death constantly hovering over them, made them undisturbed spectators of every occurrence, making the most of to-day, heedless of the morrow. Though constantly threatened with death, they pursued with eagerness limited occasions for amusement. The song and jest went around, fun actually being coined from the danger which some comrade escaped, or attempted to nimbly dodge.

The movable breastwork in front of the intrenchments of the Third Louisiana, became a perfect annoyance to the regiment, and various plans were proposed for its destruction, only to be declared unavailable. Some of the men actually proposed to make a raid on it and set it on fire, a plan which would have been the height of madness.

Lieutenant W. M. Washburn, of Company B, loaded a rifle, and fired a ball of cotton and turpentine into the hated object. Another and another blazing missile was sent on the mission of destruction, with apparently no satisfactory results, and the attempt was abandoned amid a general disappointment. The men, save those on guard, sought repose, and all the line became comparatively quiet. Suddenly some one exclaimed, "I'll be d——d if that thing isn't on fire!" The whole regiment was soon stirring about, like a hive of disturbed bees. ·Sure enough, smoke was seen issuing from the dark mass. The inventive genius of Lieutenant Washburn had proved a complete success, and the fire, which had smouldered in the dense mass of cotton, was about bursting forth. The men seized their rifles, and five companies were immediately detailed to keep up a constant and rap d fire over the top and at each end of the blazing mass, to prevent the enemy from extinguishing the flames. The Yankees could not understand how their movable breastwork was thus given to destruction under their very eyes.

June 11th, the enemy in front of the Third Louisiana planted two ten-inch Columbiads, scarcely a hundred yards distant from the lines. These terrible missiles, with their heavy scream and tremendous explosion, somewhat startled the boys, being a new and unexpected feature in the siege, and necessarily increasing the already accumulated danger of their situation. After knocking the breastworks to pieces, and exhibiting their force and power, the enemy commenced a systematic method of practice, so as to make the shells deadly missiles of destruction. The siege-guns were particularly destructive, especially among the right companies of the regiment. Our troops succeeded in getting a mortar in position, in a ravine in the rear of the line of fortifications, and opened on the Yankees in the evening. As the shell marked its graceful curve in the air, and suddenly fell into the enemy's lines, the troops cheered most vociferously. They enjoyed, to the fullest extent, the astonishment and consternation of the Yankees. But a few shells, however, were fired ere the enemy concentrated upon the point whence came the dangerous missiles, the fire of every gun within easy range pouring such a storm of shell upon the offending mortar as caused its speedy abandonment. It was almost certain death to remain in its vicinity. This mortar was used only a short time, and then the attempt to render it effective given up.

June 17th, another columbiad opened on the regiment at close range, and the enemy's lines were now so near, that scraps of paper could be thrown by the combatants into each others ranks. Thus, a Yankee threw a "hard-tack" biscuit among the men of the regiment, having written on it the word "starvation." The visitor was immediately returned, indorsed as follows: "Forty days' rations, and no thanks to you." The Vicksburg "Whig" published an extra, containing a few items concerning the siege of Port Hudson. This paper, published at intervals, was printed on one side of wall paper. It was very small, and a great curiosity in the way of a relic. It was decidedly an "illustrated" sheet, but not exactly after the style of " Frank Leslie " and " Harper's" pictorials.

June 28th, orders were issued to select the finest and fattest mules within the lines, and slaughter them, for the purpose of issuing their flesh as food to the troops; a half pound per man was the ration of this new species of flesh. Several Spaniards belonging to the Texas regiments were busily occupied in jerking this meat for future consumption. This meat was also supplied to the citizens from the market, and sold for fifty cents a pound. Mule flesh, if the animal is in good condition, is coarse-grained and darker than beef, but really delicious, sweet and juicy. Besides this meat, traps were set for rats, which were consumed in such numbers that ere the termination of the siege, they actually became a scarcity. Hunger will demoralize the most fastidious tastes, and quantity, not quality of food, becomes the great desideratum. The author made a hearty breakfast on fried rats, whose flesh he found very good.

June 29th found the enemy once more undermining the works held by the Third Louisiana Infantry, and the men went spiritedly at work digging a counter mine. The laborers were so near each other that the strokes of the pickaxes could be distinctly heard, as well as the sound of the voices. Thus the deadly struggle went on, the brave boys never once dreaming of despairing or giving up, although fighting over a volcano which at any moment might burst forth and engulf them in a general ruin. The Federal sharpshooters very impudently wished to know how we liked mule meat, proving conclusively that they were constantly informed of every event which occurred within the lines. Their question, however, was responded to in not very flattering or complimentary language. At 2 p. m. the enemy exploded the mine beneath the works occupied by the Third Louisiana Infantry. A huge mass of earth suddenly, and with tremendous force and a terrific explosion, flew upwards, descending with mighty power upon the gallant defenders, burying numbers beneath its falling fragments, bruising and mangling them most horribly. It seemed as if all hell had suddenly yawned upon the devoted band, and vomited forth its sulphurous fire and smoke upon them. The regiment, at this time, was supported by the First, Fifth and Sixth Missouri Infantry, and upwards of a hundred were killed and wounded. Numbers were shocked and bruised, but not sufficiently to more than paralyze them for a few moments. The scene that followed beggared description. At first there was a general rush to escape the huge mass of descending earth. Then the survivors, without halting to inquire who had fallen, hastened to the immense gap in the works to repel the anticipated assault. The enemy, taught by a dearly-bought experience, made no attempt to enter the opening, not daring to assault the intrepid defenders. An immense number of 12-pound shells, thrown from wooden mortars, by the Yankees, descended among the troops, doing fearful execution.

July 2d, provisions were very scarce, and murmurs of discontent began to be heard, but only among a few, whose patriotism and devotion gave way under the accumulating horrors and the gnawings of hunger. The majority of the troops were as eager as ever, undaunted and unconquered as when the enemy first appeared, expresssing a willingness and determination to hold the place as long as a mouthful of anything eatable remained to sustain life. It was the hour that tried the souls of

men. A few fleeting days must determine for succor and freedom, or defeat and capture. Provisions were becoming a rarity,
and mule flesh was freely issued and ravenously devoured. The
approaching national anniversary was looked forward to as a day
of fearful strife. The boys laughingly inquired, "We wonder
who will be the best satisfied with the grand celebration?"

The guns on the peninsula poured a rapid fire on the city, the
100-pounder Parrots doing terrible execution on the buildings.
Our batteries were very quiet. The question was frequently pro-
pounded, in view of an expected surrender, "Why not expend
our large supply of ammunition in firing upon the enemy, rather
than permit it to pass into their hands, to swell the list of their
captures?" Echo questioned, "Why?"

July 3d a flag of truce went out to the enemy's lines, and rumors began to prevail that the place was about to be surrendered.
The brave garrison indignantly denied such a contingency, yet
scarcely knew what to believe. Affairs looked very gloomy.

July 4th, a day memorable in the annals of American history,
was destined once again to be made memorable as a day both of
rejoicing and humiliation to those who had besieged and defended
Vicksburg. Early in the day it became known that negotiations
were pending for the surrender of the Southern stronghold. A
perfect storm of indignation burst forth among the troops.
What! surrender, and that, too, on the 4th of July, above all
other days? Impossible! Alas! it became too true! The following order was promulgated:

HEADQUARTERS, FORNEY'S DIVISION,
JULY 4th, 1863.

I am directed by Lieutenant-General commanding to inform
you that the terms for the capitulation of Vicksburg and garrison
have been completed, and are as follows:

The officers and men will be paroled at once, retaining their
private baggage; commissioned officers their side-arms, and
mounted officers one horse each.

At ten o'clock A. M. to-day, each brigade will be marched out
in front of its respective position, stacking arms; it will then
return, and bivouac in rear of the trenches until the necessary
rolls can be completed. You will please state to your troops that
these terms are concurred in by the general officers, and you will
caution your men not to avoid being paroled, as it is to their

advantage to have their papers properly made out. So soon as the order is received you will cause white flags to be displayed along your lines.

I am, General, very respectfully,

Your obediant servant,

J. H. FORNEY,

Official: *Major-General Commanding.*

W. D. HARDIMAN, *A. A. G.*

The receipt of this order was the signal for a fearful outburst of anger and indignation seldom witnessed. The members of the Third Louisiana Infantry expressed their feeling in curses loud and deep. Many broke their trusty rifles against the trees, scattered the ammunition over the ground where they had so long stood battling bravely and unflinchingly against overwhelming odds. In many instances the battle-worn flags were torn into shreds, and distributed among the men as a precious and sacred memento that they were no party to the surrender. The Federals who marched into the place had more the appearance of being vanquished than the unarmed Confederates, who gazed upon them with folded arms and in stern silence, a fierce defiance on their bronzed features, and the old battle fire gleaming in their glittering eyes. During all the events of the surrender, not one had been seen, and afterward no word of exultation was uttered to irritate the feelings of the prisoners. On the contrary, every sentinel who came upon post brought haversacks filled with provisions, which he would give to some famished Southerner, with the remark, "Here, reb., I know you are starved nearly to death."

SCENES AFTER THE SURRENDER.

During the siege of Vicksburg, there was a class of non-combatants who distinguished themselves in a marked manner. These were the speculators, embracing nearly every merchant within the limits of the city, without distinction of nationality. These bloodsuckers had the audacity to hold their goods at such prices that it was an utter impossibility to obtain anything for them. Four hundred dollars was the price of a barrel of flour; coffee was ten dollars per pound, and everything else in like proportion. Some of these worse than villains, refused to sell to the soldiers at any price, and, consequently, were not objects of special love by the brave men.

When the Federal soldiers entered the city they mingled freely with the Confederates, and expressed their sympathy with their deplorable situation by every possible means in their power. They were now no longer deadly combatants, but mortals of similar feelings. A retributive justice speedily descended upon the speculators, as the Federals broke open their stores, completely plundering them. The Southerners looked on this work of destruction with feelings akin to satisfaction, and felt as if a portion of their wrongs were avenged.

Wines, for which the sick had pined in vain, were brought to light; luxuries of various kinds were found in profusion. The Federals brought them into the streets, and throwing them down, would shout, "Here, rebs., help yourselves, you are naked and starving and need them." What a strange spectacle of war between those who were so recently deadly foes! Such generosity was no rarity, and softened down much of the deadly animosity and bitter feelings experienced by the vanquished for their foes. Many found friends and relatives, and the Third regiment had more than its share among the Federal troops.

Aside from the speculators, was a class of citizens in Vicksburg who did their duty nobly. Let it be known, everywhere written in ineffaceable characters upon the pages of history; traced with golden letters upon the scroll of Time ; stamped with an indelible impression upon every manly Southern heart, that the *ladies* of *Vicksburg* were as true as steel, charitable to a fault upon every occasion, where their services were needed. Flitting like ministering angels about the hospitals, giving aid and comfort to the sick and wounded; hovering with tearful eyes over the dying soldier; treading their way along the torn-up streets, amid the scream of shot and shell, and the storm of descending iron, on missions of love and mercy, they exhibited a heroism and devotion beyond portrayal by human language.

July 5th, rations for five days were issued to the Confederates from the Commissariat of the Federals. These rations consisted of bacon, hominy, peas, coffee, sugar, soap, salt, candles and crackers. How the famished troops enjoyed such bounteous supplies it is needless to state. For once the brave boys were the objects of their enemy's charity. They grew jovial and hilarious over the change in their condition. The Yankees came freely among them, and were unusually kind. They asked innumerable questions, and were horrified at the fact of the men eating mules and rats, and openly expressed their admiration for the unfaltering bravery of the Confederates.

On the 7th, the work of paroling commenced. The men were paroled separately, and subscribed to the following oath:

VICKSBURG, MISS., July 7, 1863.

To all whom it may concern:

Know ye, that I, ———— ————, a private, Company————, ————Regiment, ————Volunteers, C. S. A. being a prisoner of war in the hands of the United States forces, in virtue of the capitulation of the City of Vicksburg and its garrison by Lieutenant-General John C. Pemberton, C. S. A., commanding on the 4th day of July, 1863, do, in pursuance of the terms of said capitulation, give this day my solemn parole, under oath:

That I will not take up arms again against the United States, nor serve in any military, police or constabulary force in any port, garrison or field-work held by the Confederate States of America, against the United States of America, nor a guard of prisons, depots or stores, nor discharge any duties usually performed by officers or soldiers, against the United States of America, until duly exchanged by the proper authorities.

Sworn to and subscribed before me, at Vicksburg, Miss., this 7th day of July, 1863.

JOHN O. DUER,
Captain 40th Illinois Regiment, and Paroling Officer.

At 11:30 o'clock A. M. July 11th, the army bade a final adieu to Vicksburg. They marched out of their stronghold with a proud step, and a stern defiance on their faces. The roadsides and embankments were crowded with Federals, to take a farewell glance at the troops who had fought them so stubbornly and desperately. Not a word of exultation or an outburst of any feeling was so manifested by the foe. Honoring the heroic garrison for their bravery, they would not add to the humiliation of their surrender by a single taunt. As the Third Regiment passed out of the works which they had defended with such obstinate bravery, they saw a large detail actively engaged in filling up the approaches which they had dug to the intrenchments occupied by the regiment. The old spirit of defiance broke forth in words, as they witnessed the scene. "Oh! yes," said one, "shovel dirt, d—n

you; it is all you are good for. You can do that better than
fighting." "Dry up," retorted a Federal, "you rebels have grown
wonderful sassy on Uncle Sam's grub." It was a home-thrust,
and the boys journeyed by in silence.

SONGS.

The men often indulged their propensity for song-writing, and
if their productions did not exhibit splendid poetical talent, the
sentiments of these songs manifested the spirit which animated
them, their reckless disregard to danger, and their propensity to
make mirth out of their sufferings. It was no unusual occurrence to hear, amid the battle's fierce din, the choruses of these
songs shouted forth with stentorian voices, or their strains at
night softly floating away over the intrenchments on the quiet air.

In the following pages are given a few of these songs, which
fell into the hands of the author after the surrender of Vicksburg:

A LIFE ON THE VICKSBURG HILL.

By A. DALSHEIMER, Co. K, THIRD LOUISIANA REGIMENT.

AIR: "*Life on the Ocean Wave.*"

A life on the Vicksburg hills,
 A home in the trenches deep,
A dodge from the Yankee shells,
 And the old pea-bread won't keep.
  The bread—the bread—
 And the old pea-bread won't keep.

Like a rebel caged I pine,
 And I dodge when the cannons roar;
But give me corn dodgers and swine,
 And I'll stay forever more.

Once more in the trench I stand,
 With my own far-ranging gun;
Should the fray come hand to hand,
 I'll wager my rations I run.

The trench is no longer in view;
 The shells have begun to fall;
'Tis a sound I hate—don't you?
 Into my rat-hole I'll crawl.

The bullets may whistle by,
 The terrible bombs come down;
But give me full rations, and I
 Will stay in my hole in the ground.

Oh! a life on the Vicksburg hills,
 A home in the trenches deep,
A dodge from the Yankee shells.
 And the old pea-bread won't keep.

—10

DO THEY MISS ME IN THE TRENCHES.

----

*By J. W. Naff, Third Louisiana Regiment.

Air: "*Do They Miss Me at Home.*"

Do they miss me in the trench, do they miss me?
    When the shells fly so thickly around?
Do they know that I've run down the hill-side
    To look for my hole in the ground?
But the shells exploded so near me,
    It seemed best for me to run;
And though some laughed as I craw-fished,
    I could not discover the fun.

I often get up in the trenches,
    When some Yankee is near out of sight,
And fire a round or two at him,
    To make the boys think that I'll fight.
But when the Yanks commence shelling,
    I run to my home down the hill;
I swear my legs never will stay there,
    Though all may stay there who will.

I'll save myself through the dread struggle,
    And when the great battle is o'er
I'll claim my full rations of laurels,
    As always I've done heretofore.
I'll say that I've fought them as bravely
    As the best of my comrades who fell,
And swear most roundly to all others
    That I never had fears of a shell.

----

*Killed the day after writing this song.

'TWAS AT THE SIEGE OF VICKSBURG.

AIR: "*Mocking Bird.*"

'Twas at the siege of Vicksburg,
Of Vicksburg, of Vicksburg,
'Twas at the siege of Vicksburg,
When the Parrot shells were whistling through the air—
Listen to the Parrot shells,
Listen to the Parrot shells,
The Parrot shells are whistling through the air.

Oh! Well will we remember,
Remember, remember,
Though mule meat, June *sans* November;
And the minnie balls that whistled through the air—
Listen to the minnie balls,
Listen to the minnie balls,
The minnie balls are singing in the air.

VICKSBURG: A BALLAD.

By Paul H. Hayne.

I.

For sixty days and upwards
    A storm of shell and shot
Rained round us in a flaming shower,
    But still we faltered not!
"If the noble city perish,"
    Our grand young leader said,
"Let the only walls the foe shall scale
    Be the ramparts of the dead!"

II.

For sixty days and upwards,
    The eye of heaven waxed dim,
And even throughout God's holy morn,
    O'er christian's prayer and hymn,
Arose a hissing tumult,
    As if the fiends in air
Strove to ingulf the voice of faith
    In the shriek of their despair.

III.

There was wailing in the houses,
    There was trembling on the marts,
While the tempest raged and thundered
    'Mid the silent thrill of hearts;
But the Lord, our shield, was with us,
    And ere a month had sped,
Our very women walked the streets
    With scarce one thought of dread.

IV.

And the little children gambolled,
    Their faces purely raised,
Just for a wondering moment,
    As the huge bomb whirled and blazed!
Then turned with silvery laughter
    To the sports which children love,
Thrice mailed in the sweet, instinctive thought,
    That the good God watched above.

V.

Yet the hailing bolts fell faster,
    From scores of flame-clad ships,
And about us, denser, darker,
    Grew the conflict's wild eclipse,
Till a solid cloud closes o'er us,
    Like a type of doom and ire,
Whence shot a thousand quivering tongues
    Of forked and vengeful fire.

VI.

But the unseen hands of angels
    Those death shafts turned aside
And the dove of heavenly mercy
    Ruled o'er the battle tide;
In the houses ceased the wailing,
    And through the war-scarred marts.
The people strode, with step of hope,
    To the music in their hearts.

THE RAINBOW OF HOPE.

By W. M. WASHBURN, Co. B, THIRD LOUISIANA.

AIR: "*Life on the Wave.*"

There's the rainbow of Hope in the moonlit sky,
    Man the works! fling trembling away, my boys;
The breeze is soft, our God is on high,
    He will shield us if we are still true, my boys.
We have slept in the calm, we have laughed in the storm,
    We will sing by the bomb's red glare, my boys;
Should the foe come on, with a strong heart and arm,
    And a keen blade, we'll send him away, my boys.

And the rainbow of Hope, while it lingers still,
    We will strike for the dear ones at home, my boys,
We will trust to our blades and to God's good will,
    And fling ever fear to the winds, my boys.
We will bear every hardship, or peril, or pain,
    For our loved ones are trusting to us, my boys,
And we'll proudly return to greet them again,
    Or as proudly fill a soldier's grave, my boys.

Light hearts we bring to rescue our land,
    Though a shadow has hung o'er her of late, my boys;
We will strike for our homes with a steady hand,
    And a smile for whate'er be our fate, my boys.
Though some may sleep 'neath the hill-side sod,
    Though none go back to their homes, my boys,
Yet the hearts that are true to their country and God,
    Will all meet at the last reveille, my boys.

THE BATTLE-CRY OF FREEDOM.

———

Yes, we'll rally round the Flag, boys, we'll rally once again,
　Shouting the battle-cry of Freedom!
We will rally from the hill-side, we'll gather from the plain,
　Shouting the battle-cry of Freedom!

CHORUS.

　The Union forever! hurrah! boys, hurrah!
　　Down with the Traitor, up with the Star!
　While we rally round the Flag, boys, rally once again,
　　Shouting the battle-cry of Freedom!

We are springing to the call of our Brothers gone before,
　Shouting the battle-cry of Freedom!
And we'll fill the vacant ranks with a million Freemen more,
　Shouting the battle-cry of freedom!

　　　Chorus:　The Union forever! etc.

We will welcome to our numbers the boys all true and brave,
　Shouting the battle-cry of Freedom!
And although he may be poor, he shall never be a Slave,
　Shouting the battle-cry of Freedom!

　　　Chorus:　The Union forever! etc.

So we're springing to the call from the East and from the West,
　Shouting the battle-cry of Freedom!
And we'll hurl the Rebel crew from the land we love the best,
　Shouting the battle-cry of Freedom!

　　　Chorus:　The Union forever! etc.

RED, WHITE AND BLUE.

Oh, Columbia, the gem of the ocean,
 The home of the brave and the free,
The shrine of each patriot's devotion,
 A world offers homage to thee.
Thy mandates make heroes assemble,
 When liberty's form stands in view,
Thy banners make tyrants tremble,
 When born by the red, white and blue.

CHORUS.

 When born by the red, white and blue,
 When born by the red, white and blue,
 Thy banners make tyrants tremble,
 When born by the red, white and blue.

When war waged its wide desolation,
 And threatened our land to deform,
The ark then of freedom's foundation,
 Columbia rode safe through the storm.
With ner garland of victory o'er her,
 When so proudly she bore her bold crew,
With her flag proudly floating before her,
 The boast of the red, white and blue.
   The boast of, etc.

The wine cup, the wine cup bring hither
 And fill you it to the brim,
May the wreath they have won never wither
 Nor the star of their glory grow dim.
May the service united not sever,
 And hold to their colors so true,
The army and the navy for ever,
 Three cheers for the red, white and blue.
   Three cheers, etc.

DO THEY MISS ME AT HOME?

Do they miss me at home? do they miss me?
    'Twould be an assurance most dear
To know that this moment some loved one
    Were saying, I wish he were here!
To feel that the group at the fireside
    Were thinking of me as I roam;
Oh! yes, 'twould be joy beyond measure
    To know that they missed me at home.

When twilight approaches the season
    That ever is sacred to song,
'Does some one repeat my name over,
    And sigh that I tarry so long?
And is there a chord in the music
    That's missed when my voice is away,
And a chord in each heart that awaketh
    Regret at my wearisome stay?

Do they set me a chair near the table
    When evening's home pleasures are nigh,
When the candles are lit in tne parlor,
    And the stars in the calm, azure sky?
And when the "good nights" are repeated,
    And all lay them down to their sleep,
Do they think of the absent, and waft me
    A whispered "good night" while they sleep?

Do they miss me at home? do they miss me
    At morning, at noon, or at night?
And lingers one gloomy shade round them
    That only my presence can light?
Are joys less invitingly welcome,
    And pleasures less hale than before,
Because one is missed from the circle,
    Because I am with them no more?

APPENDIX H.

HISTORY OF VAUGHN'S CONFEDERATE BRIGADE.

BY CAPT. E. E. HOUSTON, OF GEN. J. C. VAUGHN'S STAFF.

Vaughn's East Tennessee Brigade was camped in the groves contiguous to Vicksburg, with the left of our line resting on the Mississippi river, when Grant moved down with his minions and commenced his canal across the peninsula in April, 1863. About this time a fearful storm passed over our camp, which blew down the immense poplar trees, killing sixty men in the old Third and Sixty-third Tennessee regiments. Four brothers of Monroe county, Tenn., who were sleeping together, were killed by one tree. This depressed the Tennessee troops very much, and we had quite a number to desert. However, in the course of a few weeks they got over this, and the active picket duty and the frequent alarms at the river batteries gave them but little time to think of their trouble. On the last day of April our brigade was ordered to prepare three days' rations, and march to the railroad crossing at Big Black river for further orders. Having reached this point, we were ordered to take position in the ditches in the horseshoe on the Edwards side of the river.

May 1st we heard the muttering of war. Port Gibson's battle had been fought, and the Confederate troops whipped. Next came Raymond's battle on the twelfth, Jackson the fourteenth, and Baker's Creek, or Champion Hills, on the sixteenth. In all of these our troops were whipped and scattered. In the latter fight, General Loring refused to go into the "man trap," General Pemberton not knowing where his troops were, or even the topography of the country. The U. S. troops moved direct from Champion Hills for our trenches at Black river. Vaughn, who was in immediate command of this battle, had only men enough to place one every four feet in the ditches, and though frequent application was made for more troops to mass on the left, we never got them, Pemberton being, to all appearances—so far as my judgment could determine—as helpless and undecided as a child. In the meantime, Grant's victorious forces, ten times our numbers, moved rapidly forward, and while they were checked two or three times, they soon found our unprotected left, and with one grand bound, it seemed to me, carried our whole line. Troops were retreating pell-mell to the pontoons and railroad crossing. Hundreds were captured—in fact, one whole regiment on the right; and with a mere remnant of the 3,800 men that we marched out of Vicksburg with, we returned with about two thousand for duty. In this fight I saw General Vaughn under the most terrible fire; he was cool and collected, and at one time a cannon ball cut the reins of his bridle, and while I got off my horse to tie them, he seemed unconscious of fear. Lieut. Jno. Toland was ordered to withdraw the troops, and rode up boldly to the lines and gave the orders, at one time thrown from his horse, and in order to save himself, had to swim the river, as I had turned over the barrels of turpentine, and, under orders, set fire to the boats out of which we had made a pontoon. We marched back to Vicksburg, and with feelings of the mariner who has been tempest-tossed and was about entering a safe harbor, for we firmly believed the city impregnable; and if invested, that we had food enough to last us until the armies of the Confederacy would relieve us—in fact, we were informed by general orders that we had six months' rations within the works.

The nineteenth day of May our lines were withdrawn into the inner works, and the day revealed to us that we were surrounded. The bristling bayonets on the land side, the white smoke bursting from the mortar-boats anchored on the river side, the bursting of shells and playing of iron-clads, told its tale. The brigade of General Vaughn was placed in the ditches and protection of the "upper" river batteries to "razor-back hill." The Mississippi

State troops having been placed under command of General Vaughn, their lines commenced there and extended about half a mile. As to how deep the ditches would have been dug by the time the siege was over, this deponent saith not, as these State troops were worse than gophers, for they soon had their ditches so deep that they could not reach the top of them with the muzzles of their guns, and orders had to be made for them to fill up.

In about ten days after the enemy had surrounded us, orders were issued to be careful of rations, and for their reduction. Then came a detail of a portion of a Texas regiment to jerk mule meat; then followed orders for the peas to be mixed with corn and wheat, and to be ground; these orders were carried out. The mule meat was good, and in a few days very few were heard to grumble, but the grinding of the peas seemed to have poisoned them. While you could fry them, and they tasted well enough, the stomach would not retain them at all. The troops were in moderate health; but few in the hospital; it was not safe there. Though all of Vaughn's artillery at times was disabled and use- less, still his lines were not broken during the whole siege, and we stacked arms in the ditches we had held for forty days, on the 4th of July, and saw the victorious troops file into our fortress. The victors were generous, and many were the hands I saw drawing food from their haversacks and give to our hollow-eyed and famished boys. It was about the 11th of July when all our soldiers, 32,000 in number, had been paroled and ready to leave.

APPENDIX I.

CONFEDERATE REMINISCENCES.

A Federal Shell in Vicksburg—Its Terrific Explosion in a
Confederate Hospital.

[SELECTED.]

An Exploding Shell.—At 3 o'clock A. M., June 9, 1863, a fifteen inch shell from a U. S. mortar boat struck the City Hospital. It entered the top of the building and passed through the upper stories, walls and ceilings, smashing up and destroying everything in its path. It descended into the room occupied by surgeons. Dr. Britts and Dr. Taylor, of Paducah, Ky., were in bed and asleep in the room. The shell, instead of penetrating the floor beneath, took a circuit around the room and exploded before Dr. Britts could get out of the room; but Dr. Taylor, whose bed was near the door, managed to escape before the explosion. Dr. Britts was held down and prevented from moving by a load of plastering and debris that covered him, and before he could extricate himself the shell exploded with deafening noise, and filled the room with a hundred broken fragments, accompanied by flames and a suffocating smoke.

Damage to a Surgeon.—One of the fragments from the bursted shell carried away one of Dr. Britts' legs. Another fragment pierced through his right lung, and another missile wounded him in the left knee. The doctor felt himself bleeding to death, and had presence of mind, after extricating himself, to take up the arteries and tie them, thereby preventing the flow of blood therefrom. After a while they got him out and amputated his leg. The doctor says he never lost his presence of mind, although terribly wounded, and smothered by the partition wall blown by the force of the missile. He says he experienced precisely the same sensation said to be felt by drowning men. His whole past life seemed concentrated in a few seconds, and his mind was filled with illusions of his early years, which impressed him as vividly as the reality. He felt no pain in his dismembered leg, and in fact, having been placed by his surgeon under the effect of chloroform, he experienced no pain while undergoing the amputation, and during the long months of recovery.

Among the Patients.—Elder James Bradley, of Rolling Home postoffice, Randolph county, Missouri, and Chris. Sears, of Randolph county, son of the late Judge Sears, were at the time wounded and lying on a cot on the ground floor in the room adjoining the surgeons, with many other sick and wounded Confederate soldiers. The partition wall between the two rooms was entirely blown out, and the soldiers in the room adjoining were literally buried in the debris of the falling wall. Mr. Bradley was suffering from a wound made by the explosion of a shell just as it came even with his shoulders, lacerating and wounding him very badly. Sears had a very peculiar wound, indeed. He was shot in the face with a leaden ball. The ball struck square on the bridge of the nose, and separating from some cause, came out in two places through the roof of his mouth and was taken out with his own hands. Mr. James H. Robertson, of Fayette, under whom, as editor of the *Banner*, we took our first lessons in the newspaper business, was suffering at the time from a wound in the left shoulder made by a grape shot, and was lying in the hall of the second story on a blanket at the time. The shell passed through the roof and two floors above him, and through the floor on which he lay, about four feet from him. We had often heard him speak of the circumstance, and we wrote to him about it when we saw the statement above given in the *Republican*. Mr. R. says that Dr. Whitehead, surgeon of the Third Louisiana infantry, and a number of wounded soldiers of that regiment, were in the building at the time. Eight were killed and fourteen wounded.

Other Mention.—Dr. W. A. Monroe, son of the distinguished Andrew Monroe, of the M. E. Church South, and now a prominent physician of Memphis, Mo., and Mr. George W. Riggins, afterward extracted the grape shot from Mr. R.'s shoulder, at the hospital at Greenwood, Louisiana. Dr. Riggins now resides in Columbia, and although a surgeon of acknowledged ability, has not practiced his profession for several years.

The shelling of Vicksburg from the fleet in the river, and from the guns of the Federals along the miles of breastworks at the same time, is said to have been one of the grandest and gloomiest pictures in the annals of war. Mr. Robertson says the history of the siege has never been written.—*Missouri Republican and Columbia Sentinel.*

Dr. Nidelet's Account of the Exploding Shell.—In the narrative from which the foregoing is taken, reference was made to Dr. S. L. Nidelet, of St. Louis, as having been a sharer in the exploding shell's injurious effects. On personal application to him he gave a verbal recital of the facts known to himself, which are as follows :

" The City Hospital building, used as a Confederate hospital, stood on the highest ground about Vicksburg, and was the most conspicuous target in the city for heavy shells hurled from Porter's mortar boats anchored at the river's edge on the west side of the peninsula, about three miles distant on a direct line, which were fired day or night, as suited the inclinations of the gunners and their commanders. The shells were fired at an angle which caused them to describe a circuit through the air like that of the rainbow, making the journey considerably more than three miles to the hospital. The destructive shell was conical in shape, and only about two inches less in diameter than the mouth of a flour barrel.

"It was started on its destructive mission a little after 1 o'clock A. M. Dr. Britts and I had completed the amputation of the leg of a wounded Confederate at 1 o'clock, and Dr. Britts had retired to his bed room, which was immediately below the surgery room, in the northeast corner of the building. The shell exploded upon the brick floor of the room, tearing away the major part of the north and east outer walls, and wrecking the south partition wall, portions of which fell upon Dr. Britts, whose bed was next the wall. The Doctor was wounded not only by fragments of shell, but his leg was injured by a piece of brick from the floor. His lung wounds caused an abscess to form, and he narrowly escaped death. His recovery was a marvel."

The floor of the operating room on which Dr. Nidelet was standing was blown up with such force as to lift him bodily, and force him on the top of an open door, from which he fell into a hall on the south side, into which the doorway led. A piece of shell cut his nose and another lifted his scalp, and has left an indentation where the wound was made.

Dr. Britts lives in Clinton, Henry county, Missouri, and is a member of the State Senate. Dr. Nidelet is the present coroner of St. Louis. A few years ago they met in the Coroner's office, the first time since the war; they looked at each other for a moment, and a mutual recognition was followed by a cordial embrace and deep emotion in which men are not wont to indulge.

INCIDENTS AND PERSONAL SKETCHES OF THE MISSOURI FIRST AND SECOND CONFEDERATE BRIGADES.

By R. S. BEVIER.

BATTLE OF PORT GIBSON.

> "Ensigns high advanced,
> Standards and gonfalons, 'twixt van and rear,
> Stream in the air, and for distinction serve;
> 'Twixt host and host but narrow space was left;
> A dreadful interval, and front to front
> Presented, stood in terrible array
> Of hideous length." —*Milton.*

On the morning of the first day of May, 1863, the regiment was ordered out for action. Some of our little army of seven thousand men had been engaged since midnight, and we could distinctly hear the roll of musketry. Adjutant Greenwood formed the battalions, and as I rode out I asked him, fretfully, why he had lined them with the "Third." He smiled audibly.

It was early in the day when we moved through Port Gibson, and the noble people of the old town were up and out to cheer us to the contest. Already it could be heard—the sounds at times almost dying away, as if it were the last breath of some struggling

giant, and then, trebly thundering, the mingling echoes of cannon
and musket would "swell the gale," and we would hurry faster
forward.   Soft-eyed women looked at us through their tears, and
strong old men sobbed their farewells, knowing it was the last
day for many of us.   About two miles beyond the town we struck
the unsightly hills that bristle all along this portion of the Mississippi, and climbing up and down one rugged acclivity after
another.   We at length came to a halt in an old corn field
in front of a thick canebrake, and at the foot of a steep, cane-
covered hill.   Here we lay for some hours, waiting for orders, and
listening to the semi-circle of firing that appeared to be enlarg-
ing, as if about to enclose us completely.   Col. Gause, with the
Third, and my regiment, the Fifth, comprised our force, and
we had almost concluded we were forgotten, and began to feel
like Casabianca on the "burning deck," when we were suddenly
and very disagreeably undeceived.

Bayou Pierre, a deep and turbid stream, with impassable banks
and partly filled by backwater, passes Port Gibson from the east,
and trending towards the south, forms a junction with the Mississippi some miles below Grand Gulf.   The bridge we had crossed
on entering the town, was the only means of passage over it.

Grant had landed his forty thousand men below its mouth, and
was now pushing up its banks to obtain possession of the bridge,
and thus cut off our only means of retreat.   This would be the
first step towards, and perhaps result in, the capture of the seven
thousand men, which was the sum total of Bowen's command,
and nearly all of whom were on the south side of the bayou.

Since midnight, when the attack commenced, the enemy had
been steadily driving us back, and were confident they would soon
control the *point d'appui*.   About this stage of the game—about
two o'clock p. m.—Generals Bowen and Cockrell both came to us,
and in the hearing of many of both regiments, briefly explained
the situation, and desired us to make a determined charge on the
enemy's right flank, and divert their attention from their main
object. If we could do this we would save the little army. Accordingly, we were led through the cane-brake up a steep hill, and
from the summit shown our foe, and told to "go at them."   We
did not, however, see all of them.   The two hills seemed to be
twins, and upon the top of the other, within easy range, was a

bright and glistening field battery of eight brass guns, which immediately opened upon us with destructive effect, plowing
through the ranks in every direction with shot, shell and shrapnel. Between us was a valley with a small stream meandering
through its bottom and a few stunted trees and hardy bushes
hanging over the shallow waters. On the opposite side a large
Federal brigade was drawn up to receive us, with flags fluttering
defiance, and the sheeny sunshine glittering on their bayonets
and gun barrels. A charge at double-quick was ordered; and
through the iron hail, with even alignment and the steady tread
of the drill ground, the two regiments threw themselves into the
stunted shrubbery and the bed of the little stream. Instead of
one brigade, we now found that two confronted us—either one
quadrupling our numbers—and the continuous roll of small guns
was appalling, almost drowning the fierce discharge of the artillery. The noise was so incessant that no orders could be heard;
and the bullets flew so thick that hardly a leaf or twig was left on
the bare poles of what had been a diminutive forest when we
entered it. One of the enemy's brigades became disorganized and
confused when we charged on them, shielding ourselves under the
protection of the creek banks only ten feet distant from them,
while they were on the open ground and suffered immensely from
our fire, until they broke for shelter, leaving the other brigade
still before us. The resounding echoes of the conflict extended to
the extremest limits of the lines of both armies. Grant heard it
and was astonished. He thought Loring's whole division from
Vicksburg had struck his flank, and in hot haste withdrew a large
force from his left and hurried to reinforce his threatened right.
In the meantime, while he thought he was out-flanked, we found
that we had made a fatal mistake. That which Gen. Bowen mis-
took for the right flank of the Federal army was near the centre
of that wing, and soon after he had ordered our charge, he discovered their line stretching away for nearly a mile on our left,
and rapidly closing around us. The third courier only succeeded
in reaching us to convey the order to retreat. We were willing to
receive and act on it. We had often looked anxiously to the rear
for help or for directions to withdraw. By signs only could the
"retreat" be *sounded*. Whilst we remained in the bed of the creek
the foemen overshot us; but on the brow of the hill every inch of
it was swept by both the artillery and the musketry; and there
many a brave fellow was killed or wounded.

—11

All semblance of organization was lost. The rush to the rear was active and speedy; and over the brow of the hill, for fifty feet sheer down, the two regiments tumbled, each man plowing his individual furrow through the cane-brake, to the sore distress of his person and his uniform. At the very place where we lay so long in the corn-field, our flags were again unfolded and the rallying point established. Out of the three hundred and fifty men that went into the fight, we lost over one hundred. The remnant promptly rallied round the flag. Greenwood, our brave Adjutant, was left dead; and with him, many others had paid their last devoirs to duty. Here we remained until near sundown, the enemy not seeming disposed to follow us up or push their advantage. We retired slowly, and with precision. Except that ranks were thinner, and our battalions blood-stained, powder-grimed and dusty, the army presented the same gay appearance as in the morning. Some sober faces there were. An intimate messmate, or possibly a brother, left behind. But death is such a frequent visitor in the ranks of war that he becomes a familiar acquaintance. The social festivities of Port Gibson had endeared it to us. The elegant hospitality of its people had constituted the place an oasis in the desert of our military career. It was, therefore, with sad hearts that the remnants of our regiments slowly, and for the last time, marched through the streets. Again the terrified friends were out to greet us, with tearful eyes and pale faces, wishing us God speed, and apprehending the worst of fates in their own future. We were compelled to abandon them to it, no matter how cruel that fate might be; and just as the sun was sinking below the horizon, red and ominous, its last lingering rays decking the church steeples and adorning the court house cupola, we turned from the last fond gaze at them, and plunged into the deepening shades of the woods that bordered the bayou. King Boabdil, when he paused upon the summit of the adjoining hill to take his final look at the lofty towers of Granada, and the glittering colonnades of the Alhambra, could not have felt more sad than we.

CHAMPION HILLS AND BIG BLACK.

From Port Gibson's hard-earned fight,
To Champion Hills embattled height,
At early dawn of coming light
    We rushed upon the foe.
Tattered and torn those banners now,
But not less proud each lofty brow,
    Untaught, as yet, to yield:
With mein unblanched, unfaltering eye—
Forward! where shrieking shrapnels fly,
Fleeking with smoke the azure sky
    O'er "Champion's" fated field.
                            —*Allston.*

The entire army under Gen. Pemberton, except the watchful videttes and the yawning guards, were sunk in the most profound slumber; the cold night air played with tangled locks that for a week had been strangers to a comb, and no covering overspread us to deaden the sullen, booming sound of the distant cannon that awaked us before daybreak on the 16th of May, 1863. From the 1st of the month we had experienced a most trying time— constantly on the march, fighting nearly every day, * * arrayed in line of battle at every cross road, with no stated time for rest or refreshment, we slowly receded from Bayou Pierre and neared Vicksburg, where the final struggle was to take place.

Our hasty breakfast dispatched, we lay waiting until nine o'clock, when we were moved to an old, ridgey field, where we remained for five hours under a terrific cannonading. The men were compelled to prostrate themselves as prone as an Indian devotee before Juggernaut, the balls ricocheting not two feet over them, blinding them with dirt, burying them under clods of earth, and slaughtering most of our horses. Gen. Loring's command occupied the right, Bowen the centre and Stevenson the left. The latter, at two p. m., after half an hour of continuous discharge of musketry, which rolled from end to end of their line like a succession of alarm-beats on a million of drums, began to give back, and we were ordered to move to their support. The deafening crash of battle only served to invigorate our veterans, and at a brisk double-quick they rushed to the point of danger and conflict. As we were moving with our left in front, we had to come "on left by file into line," a difficult maneuver that can only be appreciated by a tactician, and it was rendered still more hazardous by the fact that the enemy had just captured Waddell's battery, which had been left unsupported by the flight of its defenders, and at this moment opened a galling fire on the right flank of our unformed brigade. Our brave men, however, stood firm; the unbroken line was rapidly perfected, and a movement in the face of the foe rendered successful, which was almost as difficult to perform as the celebrated "oblique order" of Epaminondas at Leuctra, or of Frederick the Great at Leuthen. Our regiments were not yet all deployed when the Federals charged us, and we met them with a fierce countercharge in an old orchard. The ground was contested inch by inch, but we drove them gradually back until we gained a mile or more. During the time, they were incessantly reinforced and made repeated stands, when our nearest mounted officer would rush back for help, and, obtaining it, would move ahead until stopped by fresh men from the other side. While galloping down a steep hill, in search of the commander of a regiment that was lying idle in the rear of us, a minnie bullet struck my horse in the flank, carrying away my scabbard, and sending me tumbling helplessly to the foot of the declivity. Captain Duncannon picked me up for dead, but I soon found that to be a mistake, and on an old artillery horse I mounted, and hurried back with the idle regiment to help us. My second horse was soon shot also, to my great relief, as he was as rough "as a spur of Matterhorn," and I took it afoot. I found our brigade sorely pressed, as well as annoyed by that dread of the brave soldier, an enfilading fire of both musketry and artillery. We were masters of the field in our front for a short time only, as inquiry developed the disagreeable fact that our ammunition had all been expended, not only each man's fifty rounds, but quite an additional supply which we had taken from the cartridge boxes of the enemy. Our ordnance stores were far in the rear, by us unattainable, and time began to press us, for the Federals had brought up their whole army and were moving against both flanks and coming on our rear. With slow and sullen dignity we retired, "violently case-shotting if pricked in our rearward parts," as Carlyle says of the Russians at Zorndorff, and therefore not much annoyed, our foemen, indeed, moving out of the way, so as to give us an unobstructed passage.

The midnight hour was near at hand when the men sank heavily to rest behind the breastworks which protected the bridge over the Big Black. Early in the morning, eyes weary and blood-shot, were opened to respond to new alarm. A heavy reconnoissance approached and was driven back. We lay quietly in the trenches, munching hard-tack and uncooked corn-beef, until ten o'clock, when the grand charge was made. Our entrenchments were thrown up in the soft soil of the bottom land, shaped like a horse-shoe, with a heavy railroad embankment running through the center, and covering two bridges, which constituted our only line of retreat. The fight opened briskly, far away to our left, confined to muskets and Enfield rifles, and no attack made in our front. We were standing by our arms, idly waiting for something to do, when we were thunderstruck at the receipt of an order to "retreat; we are flanked!" Mounting the parapet, I could see through my glass the place where a Mississippi regiment had been stationed, swarming with blue-coats and hordes besides pouring over our defences. We had been flanked, or, rather, our center pierced; were enfiladed both ways, and no altenative remained but to get away from there as fast as possible. In a jumbled crowd we rushed for the bridges. It was a regular *suave-que-pent* and devil take the hindmost.

THE SIEGE OF VICKSBURG.

Yet the hailing bolts fell faster,
  From scores of flame-clad ships;
And about us, denser, darker,
  Grew the conflict's wild eclipse,
'Till a solid cloud grew o'er us,
  Like a type of doom and ire,
Whence shot a thousand quiv'ring tongues
  Of forked and vengeful fire.   —*Hayne.*

Vicksburg is situated on a tumultuous collection of sand hills, thus forming a most admirably defensible position. It overlooks a vast expanse of the great river and a mighty horseshoe-shaped bend, upon the further side of which, with a mile and a half of water and land intervening, the mortar-boats of Porter's bombard fleet were planted, drooping into every part of the city, from over the clouds, huge iron spheres that looked like big potash kettles until they burst, when they behaved as one would imagine of an ærial powder magazine. Our breastworks consisted of hastily and irregularly constructed intrenchments, circling the other side of the city with the curve of a joggled crescent, but so badly engineered that in some places an enfilading fire would sweep us for regiments in length; and in others, palings, loosely erected, would cause more damage from wooden splinters than could have resulted from iron balls.

The 19th and 22d of May were characterized by grand and desperate charges around the entire line, easily repelled by us with but little loss, but very fatal to the assailants. After that they settled down to the regular form of siege warfare, approaching like moles, through the ground in parallels, pushing their sharpshooters to the front, who ensconced themselves in innumerable rifle-pits and behind every stump and tree; and from the land side kept up a constant discharge of hot-shot, shrapnel, shell and grape, while "Porter's bombs," from over the river, with hideous screeches, cleaved the upper air.

No safe place in the corporation could be found, except behind some of the parapets where the soldiers lay, and in the deep holes which the citizens burrowed in the sandy soil and occupied as residences; even some of these were invaded by unwelcome messengers, scattering death and destruction all around. When we were "off duty," and gathered by our camp fires, the danger was as great, possibly greater, than in the trenches. On one occasion, Major Waddell and myself were sitting on the ground, engaged at dinner. I leaned back for the purpose of extracting a toothpick from my pocket, just as a baby shrapnel came dancing over the hill, and glanced slightly against the Major's temple, but strong enough, for all that, to send him to a hospital couch for a month. The little piece of "gray goose-quill," occupied as it was in a different mission from that which Cowper contemplated, saved my life, for the ball pierced the place where my head, but for that, would have been. On the day before, as a matter of both safety and comfort, the Major and myself had constructed, by excavation, a joint bed, and this, filled with leaves and covered with blankets, enabled us to slumber like kings. Towards morning a heavy rain submerged us, of which I was totally unaware until vigorously punched by his elbow, with, "Dang it all, lay still, won't you! Every time you turn over, you let in cold water."

The Federals have several times undermined our works, exploded the charges with which the mines were filled, and charged the breaches thus caused. Here we met them. One event duplicated the other; the artillery, musketry, and bursting of hand-grenades, united with the yells of the powder-grimed combatants, the cloudy pall of sulphur, smoke and dust hanging over the lurid glare of battle, constituted a scene of sublime and terrific grandeur.

The latter of these upheavals was like the sudden eruption of a volcano, elevating an immense quantity of sand, which sank back in the form of a crater, burying beneath the *debris* near a hundred of our men. Across the mouth of it was a space of some fifty feet; one side occupied by the enemy, the other by us. Both parties kept up an incessant firing of small arms, to prevent the other from occupying the fatal pit. No soldier could show himself above the surface of the parapet, under penalty of instant death. The fusilade was kept up by discharging the guns above their heads, of course, without taking any aim. At night we had a ditch dug through the wall of the crater, and, cautiously entering, found it vacant—ours by virtue of first occupation. Our conquest was of no avail unless we utilized it by discovering the exact position of the men on the other side, as a guide in the handling of our grenades. Crawling to the farther slope, I jumped my head up with a quick movement, so as to obtain a bird's-eye view, and allow no time to be aimed at. At the same moment, a Federal officer did the same thing, and we both ducked down with remarkable agility. Determined not to "give it up so," I moved a few feet to the left. He seemed inspired by a similar impulse, moving the same distance to his right, and we simultaneously bobbed up and down to each other like two dancing-jacks.

"Halloo! old fellow," says I. "Stick your head up again!"

"Nary time," he replied.

"Who are you?" I asked.

"Lieut.-Colonel Clendennin, —th Illinois, commanding relief. Who are you?"

"Lieut.-Colonel B———, commanding relief on this side. Won't you shake hands?"

"No, I guess not."

"Well, good-bye then."

"Good-bye; I'll call on you in a few days."

The glimpse I succeeded in obtaining enabled me to direct where a rampart grenade could be rolled among a whole company of sleeping Yankees; but I did not—"a little touch of nature makes us all of kin." Our friendly interview protected for that time the lives of those unconscious slumberers. The day after the surrender, I was laying in my tent in an exceedingly bad humor, when the clattering of horses feet announced some visitors and an officer introduced himself and friends. It was my quondam acquaintance of the crater with an urgent invitation to dinner, which I could not but accept; and where we had a good time and "fought our battles o'er again" much more pleasantly than in the first instance.

As early as the middle of June, the commissariat began to run low. On the ninth of that month, Capt. Albert C. Danner, Assistant Quartermaster, makes minute that "the last of our beef has been issued, bread is made only of corn, rice and beans ground and mixed into a meal; we can not possibly hold out over twenty days, even on half rations." One private barrel of wheat flour was sold for four hundred dollars. As a soup for the sick, lean mules were slaughtered and stewed, and for famished men, made a most savory pottage. When the siege commenced, it had been announced that there were provisions enough stored away to subsist the army for six months, and in less than one month, the sudden reduction and miserable quality of rations issued, did not serve to inspire confidence among the men. All the critics of this siege insist that the town could have been amply provisioned. The failure in this respect involved the loss of the city, as well as the loss of health to many a gallant soldier. After receiving rather short rations of corn bread and indifferent beef for a few days, we were somewhat surprised one day to see, among the provisions sent up, that the only supply in the way of bread was made of peas. There is no question in regard to this pea bread; it is rather a hard edible, and was made of a well known product of several of the southern States, called cow-peas, which is rather a small bean cultivated quite extensively as provender for animals. When properly and well prepared it makes a very poor vegetable for the table, though some persons profess to be fond of it. Being introduced as a ration into the army, it was always our principal and regular vegetable; occasionally we received rice and sweet potatoes. There was a good supply of this pea in the commissariat at Vicksburg, and the idea grew out of the fertile brain of some official that, if reduced to the form of meal, it would make an admirable substitute for bread. Sagacious and prolific genius!—whether General or Commissary—originator of this glorious conception—this altogether novel species of the hardest of "hard tack!" Perhaps he never swallowed a particle of it! If he did, the truth and force of these comments will be appreciated. The process of getting the pea into the form of bread was the same as that to which corn is subjected; the meal was ground at a large mill in the city, and sent to the cooks in camp to be prepared. It was accordingly mixed with cold water, and put through the form of baking; but the nature of it was such that it never got done, and the longer it was cooked the harder it became on the outside, which was natural, but, at the same time, it grew relatively softer on the inside, and upon breaking it, you were sure to find raw pea meal in the centre. The cooks protested that it had been on the fire two good hours, but it was all to no purpose; yet on the outside it was so hard that one might have knocked down a full grown steer with a chunk of it.

The great question of edible food occupied almost as much of the attention of the besieged as did the shrieking shrapnel and the thundering shell. In the *Daily Citizen* of June 30, 1863, published in the city, by J. M. Swords, on the back of figured wall paper, the editor says:

"General Pemberton has stated he would not surrender as long as a mule or dog was left to subsist on. This possible contingency caused some of our officers yesterday to try mule meat. A couple of the long-eared animals were slaughtered, dressed and cooked, and bountifully partaken of by a large company. We learn the flesh was palatable and decidedly preferable to the stringy beef of a month past, and those who tried the mule meat prefer it for regular rations.

"The editor of the *Citizen* wishes to be understood as insinuating that the above officers omitted to extend the customary courtesies to the Press, and therefore broadly assert that mule meat would not 'go bad.' "

As a fair compensation to the poverty of the mess-pot and the skillet, came the many rose-colored rumors that seemed to float in the very atmosphere, freighted with that—

"Hope which springs eternal in the human breast,
And relieves from war the surcharged heart."

A system of communications with the outer-world was established through the medium of bold and daring couriers, who floated on planks down the river, or glided through the jungles of malarious swamps. By this imperfect mail line Bowen received his commission as Major-General. Pemberton got dispatches from Johnston, and a myriad of reports followed the arrival of each messenger. On the twenty-eighth of May General Pemberton issued a circular in which he informed the soldiers that General Joseph E. Johnston was at Canton with a large force, Loring at Jackson with ten thousand men, and that the major portion of General Bragg's army was on the move from Tennessee to reinforce Johnston, and ere long relief would be at hand. That it was also reported from the East that General Lee had whipped and driven Hooker over the Potomac, the Federals losing eighty thousand men; that Long Bridge was burned and Arlington Heights in possession of the Virginians. These rumors inspired the army with new feelings, and hope again flamed high. This was supplemented on the eleventh of June by the cheering information, received over the "grape-vine telegraph," that Price was certainly in possession of Helena, Arkansas, and held control of the Mississippi; that Bragg was occupying Memphis, and thus had closed Grant's communication with the North; that Lee was undoubtedly shelling Washington City from Arlington Heights; that Kirby Smith was positively known to be at New Carthage, Louisana; that there was no question of the fact that Semmes, with a formidable fleet of iron-clad vessels, had demolished Farragut, recaptured New Orleans and was moving up the river in concert with Magruder and Dick Taylor, expecting soon to capture Banks and his army, preparatory to finishing Grant and Porter; and finally, that the Lincoln government was suing for peace. But the reports which most persistently kept possession of the mess-talk were of Johnston's immediate advance, toward the last, daily reported more reliable, he had crossed Big Black, demolished Grant's wagon train, defeated Sherman and McClernand, was closely pressing the enemy, would soon be with us, and might hourly be expected to raise the siege. The desire to hear from General Johnston reached a feverish intensity. From a thousand hearts the wish for his appearance was often expressed as fervently as was Wellington's aspiration, "Oh, that night would come—or Blucher!"

In the meantime the siege was closely pressed, the parallels approaching in places within a few feet of each other, so the men could converse across the parapets. I know of very few instances where this mutual confidence was abused, the men in many instances mounting the works and exchanging the news, giving due notice when orders were received to fire, with, "Lie down, Rebs., we're going to shoot," or, "Squat, Yanks, we must commence firing again." A part of the warfare resolved itself into throwing over hard clods, rocks and hand grenades. The latter were small shells filled with little bullets, probably larger than a buck-shot. In return for the hand-grenades we threw shells varying from six to ninety pounds into their works, many of which did great execution; but we did not know it at that time, and this sort of shelling was not kept up; it was only after the siege that we learned that if it had been sustained, especially with the heavy shells, their nearer works would have been untenable.

The Confederate fort on the Jackson road was blown up by the explosion of a mine by the enemy on the twenty-fifth. It was situated just to the left of that road, and in its destruction we lost a number of men. The Federals charged immediately and attempted to pass through the opening, and a severe and bloody contest occurred between the hostile force and the Third Louisiana and Sixth Missouri. Col. Erwin, commanding the latter, was killed while gallantly defending the breach with his regiment. He was a brave officer, and a gentleman of talent and genius. Gen. Martin E. Green, commanding the Second Missouri Brigade, which had been in the intrenchments nearly all the time, and where he had almost exclusively remained, rarely ever leaving the ditches, was killed on the twenty-seventh of June, while reconnoitering one of the enemy's batteries. He was struck in the head by a musket ball and died instantly; and thus the life of this gray-haired patriot and brave chieftain was given to his country and to a cause for which he had long and devotedly struggled.

At twelve o'clock on the first of July our regiment—(Anderson's account of the Second Missouri infantry)—retired to its position when off duty, a little over a hundred yards back in the hollow; the Sixth Missouri was placed on duty in our stead. We had just stacked arms and entered the holes, some had taken their boots off, others their pants, as it was very warm, and were arranging to be comfortable for the time, when the ground heaved as if by an earthquake. Had the mine under the parapet been sprung? No sound immediately accompanied this motion. Was it Old Enceladus, the son of Earth, stirred in his mighty caverns? But in an instant more the terrific thunder of the explosion reached us. The elements shook at the appalling sound. The earth trembled as beneath the giant tread of Titans hurling their huge missiles against the arc of heaven. Immense columns of earth and shattered fragments ascended into the air and darkened the heavens. We seemed to stand upon the brink of a volcanic crater, ready to engulf us in its fiery flood. Simultaneously the concentrated fire of more than fifty pieces of artillery opened upon this devoted position. The furies rode in triumph around the wild chaos, and the god of war waved his gleaming sword above the raging battle. Rushing to get my gun, the first man I observed was Alford, waving his sword and commanding the men to fall into line. The regiment was quickly formed and hastened to the scene. We were met by Cockrell, who was not very far from the parapet where the explosion occurred, and with many others was blown up. He fell some distance down the hill, and miraculously escaped without any fatal injury. Though still suffering, he was very much excited, and greeted the head of the regiment in a loud and animated tone: "Forward, my brave old Second Missouri, and prepare to die." Before reaching the lines we encountered many fearful evidences of the frightful and terrible character of the affair, men being borne back by the infirmary corps, whose faces and hands presented a charred, blackened and swollen appearance, truly shocking and most horrible. Upon arriving at the ruins the sight presented to our view was frightful. Men were lying around in every direction, of whom some had been maimed and mangled, and were still living, while others were dead or lifeless—most of them dead. Those that were blown beyond the immediate circle of the explosion, which occupied a large space, were being gathered up where they were in sight. Many were covered and buried beneath the falling earth and wreck, and men were already engaged in digging for the bodies, to save, if possible, those in whom life might not yet be extinct. This labor was performed under a heavy fire, and was rewarded by finding a few living, who were immediately borne off on litters, while as rapidly as they were exhumed the most of them unfortunately were laid aside—deposited with the dead. As each body was brought forth from this living tomb it underwent its brief examination—the search for life or death. Above, around and amidst this scene of woe and death, the enemy's balls and shells whizzed and flashed in wild riot and with fatal des'ruction. Our position was immediately in rear of the ruins. The shelling was severe—fearful! Under any ordinary circumstances the post would have been considered untenable, but now it must be maintained, for every moment it was thought the artillery would cease and a charge be made. From the hostile works immediately upon the outside of our lines a small mortar had opened, throwing a twelve pound shell, and every one lighted and exploded in our mids*, rarely failing to kill or wound one, probably several of the men. Our situation was the most trying to which troops can be exposed; subjected to a deadly fire without the chance of returning it or striking the foe; for our artillery at this part of the line, confronted by vastly superior metal both in weight and number, had been dismounted or crippled, and not a single piece responded to the incessant roar of the enemy's guns. The bearing of the men never attracted my admiration more than under the circumstances in which they were now placed. The large shells from the heavy batteries, striking the top of the blown-up fortifications, burst immediately in our faces, killing and disabling the men and almost covering us with earth; but, shaking themselves and closing up the ranks, they stood devotedly to their places, and through the smoke of battle, upon every countenance was depicted the determination to hold the parapet or die in its defence. We were kept in position here for two hours, holding ourselves in readiness to receive a charge.

The artillery at last ceased firing for awhile, but the destructive little mortar still continued to play upon us with serious effect; about forty men of the regiment were struck by it, and more of them were killed than wounded. Among the last casualties of the day was Lieut.-Col. Senteney, of the Second, who was looking over the works and making some observations, when he was shot through the head by a Minnie ball and killed instantly.   With bitter tears of grief and sorrow the regiment beheld the body of this gallant officer, who had led them through many trying scenes and fiery ordeals, now borne back a corpse.

On the second of July, Captain Covell writes : "Our last rations are in our haversacks—mule meat at that.   All hope of outside relief has been abandoned.   It is said that Col. Cockrell proposed to 'cut out,' offering to lead the charging column with the Missourians, but the coils were drawn too closely, and nothing was left but surrender."

The preliminary note for terms was dispatched on the third of July.   Correspondence on the subject continued during the day, and was not concluded until nine o'clock the next morning. General Pemberton afterwards came out and had a personal interview with Grant in front of the Federal line, the two sitting for an hour and a half in close communion.   A spectator says : "Grant was silent and smoking, while Pemberton, equally cool and careless in manner, was plucking straws and biting them, as if in the merest chit-chat."   It was a terrible day's work for such display of *sangfroid*.   It was the loss of one of the largest armies which the Confederates had in the field ; the decisive event of the Mississippi Valley ; the virtual surrender of the great river, and the severance of the Southern Confederacy.   Weakness from fatigue, short rations and heat, had left thousands of the troops decrepit ; six thousand of whom were in the hospitals, and many of them were crawling about in what should have been convalescent camps ; four thousand citizens and negroes, besides Pemberton's army, including all the souls within the walls of Vicksburg.   When we consider that these people had, for a month and a half, been in daily terror of their lives, never being able to sleep a night in their homes, but crawling into caves, unable to move except in the few peaceful intervals in the heat of the day, we may appreciate what a life of horror was theirs.

From across the opposite side of the peninsula, Porter's bomb fleet maintained an active warfare, and forced upon the noncombatants unique methods of protection.   The streets were filled with excavations made by the falling and explosion of his huge missiles, and the people of the town had provided themselves with holes in the neighboring sandy hills, amid which they sought refuge during the emeny's heaviest bombardments.   These holes, or underground houses, were of considerable extent, and frequently had several rooms in them, which were provided with beds and furniture—frequently carpeted—and were, for the time, the principal abodes of many of the inhabitants. They had already been bombarded at different periods, for some months by the fleet, now lying in sight, both on the opposite side of the peninsula and below, at the mouth of the canal, and had also been attacked by forces from the land. They had become familiar with the deafening thunder of the mortar boats, and accustomed to the loud and terrific explosions of their massive shells, many of which ornamented the gate-posts of the citizens. The weight of these shells varied from a hundred and twenty-eight to two hundred and forty pounds. They were thrown high in the air from a distance of four miles, describing nearly a half-circle in their flight, and either bursted into large fragments hundreds of feet above the earth, or, failing to explode, buried themselves deep in its surface, where they frequently blew up and tore immense holes in the ground, or, the fuse having been extinguished, remained whole and self-deposited in these silent and undisturbed recesses. No more beautiful pyrotechnics could be seen than Porter's bombs as they came hissing from beyond the peninsula. At night the shelling by these mortars presented a grand display —luminous and brilliant as tropical stars—shooting the sky in lofty parabolas, and exploding to scatter their fragments over the city with vicious shrieks. Thrown from four miles away, at an angle of forty-five degrees, the fuses trailed in bright lines behind the iron monsters as they rose higher and higher in their aerial flight, like vast October meteors, until, finally, bursting among the very stars, their dazzling coruscations of brilliancy and splendor were followed by sombre gloom and the hateful whirr of the jagged iron, as it hurtled to the earth—perhaps finding a harmless grave—possibly hurrying a human being into his last resting place.

General Pemberton had issued an order, or rather a request, to the people, especially the women, who were not inclined to incur the dangers and inconvenience of a siege, to remove from the town, and he would ask of General Grant to pass them through his lines—a request which he had no doubt would be acceded to; but very few, if any, seemed inclined to leave, and they remained to share the fate of the army and abide the fortunes of their beloved city. The sick and wounded had become crowded in the hospitals; and in them were seen the forms of women, clad in simple, dark attire, with quiet steps and pale faces, gliding about and hovering around the beds of the sick and wounded; they seemed to know no cessations in their days and nights of watchfulness and care. Without noise, without display, meekly and faithfully they went forth upon their pious and holy mission, like ministering angels, carrying balm and healing to the poor soldier; cheering his hope of recovery, or soothing the last moments of expiring life. Their noble and christian devotion to the cause of suffering humanity throughout the South, during the war, can never be forgotten.

At four, a. m., of the 22d of May, a furious cannonading was opened by the enemy. This continued against the stockade until eleven o'clock, tearing off great splinters and doing much damage among the men, when a heavy force made a charge upon it. About fifty men, carrying scaling ladders, advanced to the ditch, planted their colors on the outer edge of the parapet, but finding the fire insupportable, and unable to retreat, they took refuge in the bottom of the trench. Here they were out of range, but Lieutenant K. H. Faulkner performed the perilous feat of lighting the fuse of bomb-shells and throwing them over, killing and wounding twenty-one of them. The rest escaped at night, carrying their darling flag with them. The fierceness of the fight may be judged when it is known that the Third Missouri infantry, although protected by breastworks, lost fifty-six men in killed and wounded, and each other regiment in proportion. The conflict was continued for nearly five hours, and the shades of the forest were lengthened by the setting sun, when the dispirited and discomfited enemy abandoned the attempt at storming the works, the last general attack they ventured on during the siege. Their charge was made by their whole army along our entire line, while the bombardment from over the river was kept up with spasmodic vigor. At only one point, which was Baldwin's Ferry road, did the Yankees succeed in effecting a lodgment in our works, a section of which they took, with many lusty "regulation" cheers, but, alas! for them, Green's men were coming. It was the point behind which the Second Brigade was lying, and its grey line dashed up the hill, without a shot, with bayonets fixed, and literally *pitched* the Federals over the parapet into the trench, and then leisurely shot them as they ran. The loss of the Second Brigade on this day was very small. The uniformity of incidents now became almost monotonous, as the siege drew its slow length along, and its further history is resolved into a detail of casualties and an account of resources hourly narrowing. Each day presented a succession of fighting; the ringing of rifles, the thunder of artillery, the incessant explosion of shells, saluted the ear as a morning reveille, and lulled it in the hours of sleep. The enemy, from his endless hosts, was enabled to maintain constant reliefs, nor night nor day knew any change or interruption in his ceaseless fire. The Federals continued to prosecute the siege vigorously. From night to night, and from day to day, a series of works was presented; secure and strong lines of fortifications appeared; redoubts, manned by well-practiced sharpshooters, were thrown out to the front; parapets, blazing with artillery, crowned every knoll and practicable elevation around; oblique lines of intrenchments, finally running into parallels, enabled the untiring foe to push his way slowly but steadily forward. The work of strengthening the fortifications on both sides was hourly going on; and whenever the heavy batteries of the besiegers tumbled the earth from the crest of our works, they were immediately repaired and made stronger. As the siege rolled on the enemy's efforts to reduce the city redoubled; the thunder and roar of artillery, both night and day, were incessant, and the rattle of musketry was unremitting.

SURRENDER.

Take down that banner; 'tis tattered;
Broken is its shaft, and shattered;
And the valiant hearts are scattered
    O'er whom it floated high.
Oh! 'tis hard for us to fold it—
Hard to think there's few to hold it—
Hard that those who once unrolled it,
    Now must furl it with a sigh.
             —*Miss Dinnies.*

Beautiful masses of clouds flecked the azure sky, through which the sun was sending down the fervid heat of a Southern July. The unceasing roar of the bombardment had almost become music to us, and lulled us in our very slumbers, so that when, on the 3d, a slight hush occurred, my attention was at once attracted. To the right of me, a white handkerchief, attached to a ramrod, was fluttering in the breeze, and behind, grimly awaiting the result, stood Pemberton and his staff. Soon silence settledon the scene; the "confusion worse confounded" that had prevailed all around the circle from the crescent to the river, gave place to a sweet, serene, quiet summer day—lovely with the slight haze of white smoke drifting slowly away. The blue tint of distant hills, and the far-off Louisiana woods, made all nature look pure and innocent. For forty-eight days we had been fighting, and hardly caught a glimpse of each other, save hurriedly and beneath the black smoke of a charge or the rush of a retreat.

Now the two armies stood up and gazed at each other with wondering eyes. Winding around the crests of hills—in ditches and trenches hitherto undreamed of by us—one long line after another started into view, looking like huge blue snakes coiling around the ill-fated city. They were amazed at the paucity of our numbers; we were astonished at the vastness of theirs. As the magic touch of Ithuriel's spear caused Satan, when "squat like a toad" in Paradise, to assume his true and gigantic stature, so this slight linen appurtenance of Pemberton's Adjutant brought to view the anaconda that had encircled us within its capacious folds. We recognized acquaintances and fellow-countrymen in the opposing host; and as I recalled the friendships of olden days, I remembered that sentence in the ærial invocation of Volney's Genius of the Ruins: "What accents of madness strike my ear? what blind and perverse delirium disorders the spirits of the nation?" Their parallels, in many places, had been pushed to within twenty feet of us. Conversation was easy, and while the leaders were in consultation, the men engaged in the truly national occupation of "swapping" whatever our poor boys could muster to stake a "dicker" on for coffee, sugar and whisky. None supposed the result of the official interview would be the striking of our gallant flag, and when that *was* known, the curses of our men were both loud and deep.

On the Fourth of July, like the funeral *cortege* of some renowned chieftain, our brigade moved out of our battered defenses, stacked arms, and laid across them the battle-scarred banners that "had flitted as they were borne" through a hundred fights. Dismissing the regiment, I rode into the city to see the vast Federal fleet come down to the landing, with pennons and streamers fluttering, and blaring music and blowing whistles, evidently in gayer spirits than we were.

APPENDIX J.

ARMY CORPS BADGES,

FIRST CORPS.

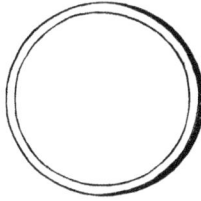

A SPHERE.

SECOND CORPS.

A TREFOIL.

THIRD CORPS.

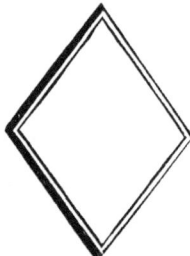

A LOZENGE.

FOURTH CORPS.

AN EQUILATERAL TRIANGLE.

FIFTH CORPS.

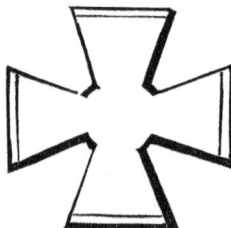

A MALTESE CROSS.

SIXTH CORPS.

A GREEK CROSS.

SEVENTH CORPS.

A CRESCENT ENCIRCLING A STAR.

EIGHTH CORPS.

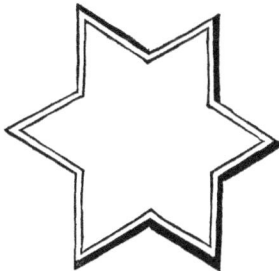

A STAR WITH SIX RAYS.

184   THE SIEGE OF VICKSBURG.

NINTH CORPS.

A SHIELD, WITH CANNON AND ANCHOR IN CENTRE.

TENTH CORPS.

THE TRACE OF A FOUR-BASTIONED FORT.

ELEVENTH CORPS.

A CRESCENT.

FOURTEENTH CORPS.

AN ACORN.

FIFTEENTH CORPS.

A MINIATURE CARTRIDGE BOX.
(Set transversely on a square.)

SIXTEENTH CORPS.

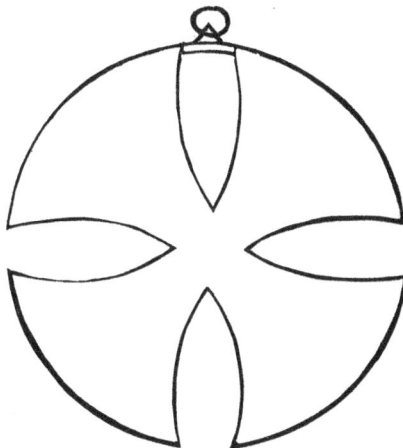

A CIRCLE, WITH FOUR MINIE-BALLS.

SEVENTEENTH CORPS.

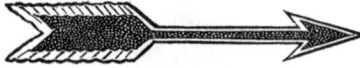

AN ARROW.

EIGHTEENTH CORPS.

A CROSS, WITH FOLIATE SIDES.

NINETEENTH CORPS.

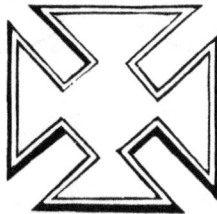

A FAN-LEAVED CROSS, WITH OCTAGONAL CENTER.

TWENTIETH CORPS.

A STAR.

TWENTY-SECOND CORPS.

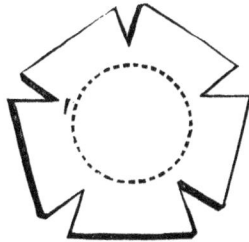

QUINQUEFOLIATE IN SHAPE, WITH CIRCLE IN THE CENTER.

TWENTY-THIRD CORPS.

A SHIELD.

TWENTY-FOURTH CORPS.

A HEART.

TWENTY-FIFTH CORPS.

A SQUARE.

The corps badges were adopted by orders from the different army headquarters, and are recognized by the Revised Statutes of the United States, as follows:

"SECTION 1,227. All persons who have served as officers, non-commissioned officers, privates, or other enlisted men, in the regular army, volunteer or militia forces of the United States during the war of the rebellion, and have been honorably discharged from the service, or still remain in the same, shall be entitled to wear, on occasions of ceremony, the distinctive army-badge ordered for or adopted by the army corps and division respectively in which they served."

When army corps were consolidated, the badges were combined as follows :

FIRST AND FIFTH CORPS.

THIRD TO THE SIXTH.

The Eleventh and Twelfth Corps were consolidated with the Twentieth, and the latter adopted the two badges.

HANCOCK'S FIRST CORPS—VETERAN VOLUNTEERS.

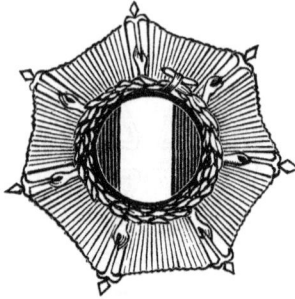

SHERIDAN'S CAVALRY CORPS.
(Worn by Commissioned Officers.)

WILSON'S CAVALRY CORPS.

FRONTIER CAVALRY.

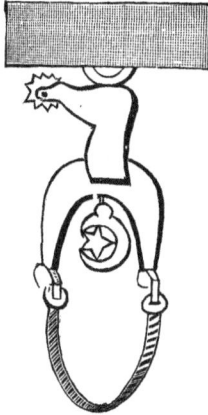

ENGINEER AND PONTONIER CORPS.

SIGNAL CORPS.

Two flags crossed, with a flaming torch between them. The flags were used in signaling by day and the torch by night.

DEPARTMENT OF WEST VIRGINIA.

ORIGIN OF SOME OF THE CORPS BADGES.

TENTH CORPS.

The service of the Tenth Corps, under Gen. Terry, in reducing the forts on the seaboard, suggested this badge.

FOURTEENTH CORPS.

Rosecrans' army, at Chattanooga, had great difficulty in getting supplies. The Fourteenth Corps was encamped near a wood of oak trees, which were at that time covered with acorns. As the rations fell short, many of the men gathered the acorns and ate them roasted, till at length it was observed that they had become quite an important part of the ration, and the men of the corps jestingly called themselves "Acorn Boys." Receiving an order about that time which required the adoption of a corps badge, the acorn was selected by acclamation.

FIFTEENTH CORPS.

Before the Fifteenth had any badge, an Irishman belonging to it went to the river near camp to fill his canteen. There he met a soldier of one of the newly arrived corps from the Eastern army, whose badges were the subject of ridicule by his comrades. The latter saluted the Irishman with the query, "What corps do you belong to?" "The Fifteenth, sure." "Well, then, where is your badge?" "My badge, is it? Well (clapping his hand on his cartridge-box), here's my badge—forty rounds! It's the order to always have forty rounds in our cartridge-boxes, and we always do."

SEVENTEENTH CORPS.

Gen. M. F. Force suggested the arrow to Gen. Frank P. Blair, commanding the corps, giving the meaning as follows: "In its swiftness, in its surety of striking where wanted, and in its destructive powers when so intended." Gen. Blair adopted it, adding, laughingly, "The arrow denotes their swiftness, the point their firmness whenever they strike, and the feathers their liking for chickens."

TWENTY-FOURTH CORPS.

Major-General John Gibbon, in his orders adopting the badge, says: "The symbol selected is one which testifies our affectionate regard for all our brave comrades—alike the living and the dead—who have braved the perils of this mighty conflict, and our devotion to the sacred cause, a cause which entitles us to the sympathy of every brave and true heart, and the support of every strong and determined hand. The Major-General commanding the corps does not doubt that soldiers who have given their strength and blood to the fame of their former badges will unite in rendering the present one even more renowned than those under which they have heretofore marched to battle."

TWENTY-FIFTH CORPS.

This corps, the first to occupy Richmond, was composed entirely of colored soldiers. Major-General Godfrey Weitzel, in his order adopting the square, says: "In view of the circumstances under which this corps was raised and filled, the peculiar claims of its individual members upon the justice and fair dealing of the prejudiced, and the regularity of the conduct of the troops which *deserve* those *equal* rights that have hitherto been denied the majority, the commanding general has been induced to adopt the *square* as the distinctive badge of the Twenty-fifth Army Corps. Wherever danger has been found and glory to be won, the heroes who have fought for immortality have been distinguished by some emblem to which every victory added a new lustre. They looked upon their badge with pride, for to it they had given its fame. In the homes of smiling peace it recalled the

—13

days of courageous endurance and the hours of deadly strife, and it solaced the moment of death, for it was a symbol of a life of heroism and self-denial.   Soldiers! to you is given a chance, in this spring campaign, of making this badge immortal.   Let history record that, on the banks of the James, thirty thousand freemen not only gained their own liberty, but shattered the prejudice of the world, and gave to the land of their birth peace, union and glory."

"Under the sod and the dew,
Waiting the judgment day;
Love and tears for the Blue,
Tears and love for the Gray."

INDEX.

PERSONAL DIARY.

*T*O THE SOLDIERS OF THE LATE WAR.

THE author of this book makes his residence in the old home of Abraham Lincoln, at Springfield, Ill. He has devoted a large portion of the building to the display of a very extensive collection of personal and historical relics of the martyred President, and articles of various kinds connected with the war of the rebellion. The different portraits, medallions, busts, engravings, autograph letters, papers, books, pamphlets, etc., of Mr. Lincoln, alone, number into thousands. No such collection as this exists anywhere in the wide world, yet you are invited to call at any time when visiting the State Capital, and examine this collection *free of charge*. If any one has a book, paper, picture, portrait or autograph of any officer, pamphlet, shot, shell, or relics of the war which they would like to add to this museum, their offering will be received with thanks, and proper credit given the donor.

LINCOLN MEMORIAL ALBUM-IMMORTELLES:

Original Contributions from the Hands and Hearts of Eminent
Americans and Europeans. Contemporaries with
the Great Martyr to Liberty. Collected
and Edited by

OSBORN H. OLDROYD,

[Author of the Siege of Vicksburg.]

WITH AN INTRODUCTION BY

MATTHEW SIMPSON, D.D. LL.D.

And a SKETCH OF LINCOLN'S LIFE,

By HON. ISAAC N. ARNOLD,

Accompanied by extracts from the speeches and recollected sayings of Abraham
Lincoln, chronologically arranged from 1832 until his death, and with
Anecdotes, Wise Words and Incidents related by the friends
of his early life.

TESTIMONIALS.

Chicago Inter-Ocean.—If every young man in the land could read these estimates
of the Nations martyred president, it would be well. It is a book which will adorn
the best library, and will be found as valuable as a book for reference as it is beautiful as a souvenir of the Nation's most honored son.

Chicago Saturday Evening Herald.—The plan of the work is novel in the extreme,
but as its development has resulted in a volume of far more than ordinary interest,
Mr. Oldroyd must be credited with a success which distinctly comprehends both
conception and execution.

New Orleans Item.—The story and lesson of his life are crystalized in a thousand
forms in the Lincoln Memorial Album, so handsomely prepared and edited by that
devoted admirer of the martyr President, Mr. O. H. Oldroyd, of Springfield, Ill.

New York Times,—There is a large number of persons who will be glad to read
this excellent sentiment over and over again for the better part of the 600 pages.

The Daily Denver News.—The universal comment of the press upon this book are
to the effect that it has met with greater favor than any book published for many
years.

Benson J. Lossing.—The contents of the Lincoln Memorial Album form a precious
offering to the memory of the martyr President. I am sure every American who
may become acquainted with the book will thank Mr. Oldroyd for its conception and
its successful production.

Admiral David D. Porter.—It is very interesting and takes a prominent place in
the history of the rebellion.

Mr. O. H. Oldroyd:—Your book is full of interest. You have done a good work
in compiling and preparing it.   M. SIMPSON.

Mr. O. H. Oldroyd: Dear Sir:—I have your delightful volume on Lincoln. It is a
treasure.   THEO. L. CUYLER.

I et a mother of an American lay this book in her boy's hands saying never a
word, and she will rear an apostle of freedom.   ROB'T MCINTYRE.

English Cloth, Gold and Black Enameled, - - - **$3.00**
Strongly Bound in Sheep—Library Style, - - - **4.00**
Beautifully Bound in Half Turkey Moroco, Marbled Edges, 5.00
Elegantly Bound in Full Turkey Morocco, Gilt Edges, - **6.00**

SOLD ONLY BY SUBSCRIPTION.

☞This book can only be obtained from our duly appointed Agents, or by
addressing

O. H. OLDROYD, Publisher,

Special Inducements to Agents.   SPRINGFIELD, ILL

THE SIEGE OF VICKSBURG.

English Cloth, Gold and Black Enameled, - - **$1.50**
Full Turkey Morocco, - - - - - **2.50**

OTHER CIVIL WAR TITLES FROM DSI

HERNDON'S LINCOLN: The True Story of a Great Life

as published in 1888

Price: $29.95

ISBN 158218108X

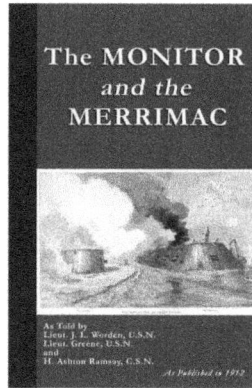

THE MONITOR AND THE MERRIMAC

as published in 1912

Price: $11.95

ISBN: 158218836X

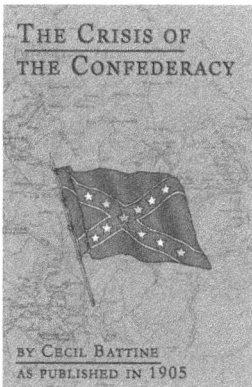

THE CRISIS OF THE CONFEDERACY

as published in 1905

Price: $21.95

ISBN: 158218674X

ADVENTURES OF ALF WILSON

as published in 1897

Price: $14.95

ISBN: 1582187894

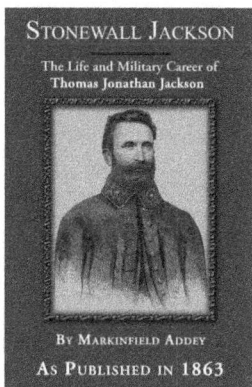

STONEWALL JACKSON

as published in 1863

Price: $12.95

ISBN: 1582183503

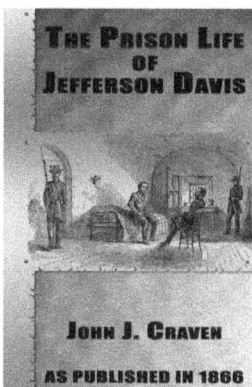

PRISON LIFE OF JEFFERSON DAVIS

as published in 1866

Price: 19.95

ISBN: 1582185107

www.ingramcontent.com/pod-product-compliance
Lightning Source LLC
Chambersburg PA
CBHW032054080426
42733CB00006B/275